MIKE'S MEMORIES

MIKE & MARGIE HUMPHRY

First published in Australia in 2022
by Mike & Margie Humphry

ISBN: 978-0-646-85163-1 (paperback)

This is a work of creative non-fiction. All of the events in this memoir are true to the best of the author's memory. Some names and identifying features have been changed to protect the identity of certain parties. The author in no way represents any company, corporation, or brand mentioned herein. The views expressed in this memoir are solely those of the author.

Design and layout by Ilura Design
www.ilurapress.com

Printed and bound by Lightning Source Australia

There have been many people who, over the past months, have been only too happy to help when I mentioned my book. However, there are two very special people I would like to acknowledge.

The late Ashley Mallett – a former Australian test cricketer, a writer, a journalist and a born story-teller. It was Ashley who took the time to advise me on how to go about writing "My Memories". He was generous in his assistance (despite the fact he was unwell and finishing a book of his own). If it had not been for Ash and his interest, I doubt my book would have seen the light of day!

Later, Diana von der Borch-Garden's knowledge, interest and assistance was invaluable in guiding me along the way. With a degree in English and Drama, a freelance writer for children's TV and a published poet, Diana also found time to write her first book. Her biographical novel, "The Second Son", based on the life of her great-grandfather, was released in 2017. Diana, who is currently writing another book while also working as a counsellor, still managed to find time to assist me in negotiating the 'pitfalls of publishing'.

CONTENTS

MEMORIES

After thirty-eight years in television, working on more than one thousand Outside Broadcasts, I have many memories. Most good, some not so good.

Some are still in sharp focus and some merging into the fog of the past.

Some are stored permanently on film or as a collection of ones and zeros.

When we are gone we exist only in the corners of the minds of others.

Here are some of those memories.

ROTTNEST

Audio Operator Lindsay Smith was dumped in the Indian Ocean more than five miles from the nearest dry land. He was being battered by huge waves and dragged even further out to sea by strong currents.

Lindsay was a big man but there was little he could do about this predicament. It was just starting to get dark – often believed to be the feeding time for the large white pointer sharks that patrolled the coast. The water was cold, and waterlogged clothes and shoes made swimming difficult.

As another huge wave loomed towards him, he could see a dark shape in the water.

Panic turned to relief when he could see the dark shape was the deckhand for the Rottnest Island Ferry! Both of them had been washed overboard by a giant wave!

For a minute they wondered if anyone had seen them go overboard. It could be a long time before someone realised they were missing. Two heads bobbing in the water would be hard to see. Then they saw the ferry begin to turn around. This involved the vessel turning side-on to the waves – thus feeling the full force of the stormy water!

Inside the ferry, Cameraman Russell Sage, the makeup artist and the dancers were hanging on to anything which was bolted down!

It took ten minutes to turn the ferry around and return to the two men! Once back on board they were dried off and given some dry clothes. Back at Fremantle they were taken to the local hospital for a check-up.

This was the end to a day of recording segments for a variety show called "In Perth Tonight"!

What a way to end the day!

Brian Williams (Director), "Johno" O'Callahan (Outside Broadcast Supervisor) and I (Technical Director) had arrived a day earlier by Army Duck at Rottnest Island to survey the island for suitable locations.

ROTTO'! Teenage memories came flooding back:

- Sleeping in a hammock in the camping grounds.
- Waking to the call of a murder of crows "ARK … ARK … ARK … STAAARK". That just happened to be the name of the Island Manager! We would imitate the call as we passed his office.
- Breakfast at the Island Bakery … Then a few games of billiards behind the General Store!

Outside Broadcast van arrives at Rottnest Island by Army Duck

- As the day warms up, we fight off the flies to get to "the Basin" for a swim. But first, check for bluebottles! Afterwards lie in the sun with no thought of skin cancer. We were invincible!
- When the sun goes down it's time to head for the Island's hotel for a few glasses of Swan or EB (Emu Bitter).
- A quokka hops past the huge Morten Bay fig trees looking for a generous person willing to share their food.

That was then, this is now.

We are on the Island to record segments for "In Perth Tonight".

We brought with us a one-camera Outside Broadcast van.

The van had a PYE 3 inch IO (Image Orthicon) camera and an RCA TR5 videotape machine in a 4WD International Harvester vehicle. The van belonged to TVW Channel 7 Perth.

I began work at TVW in 1964 while studying Electronics part-time at the Western Australian Institute of Technology after switching from a Science course at the University of WA.

Initially my job was to assist in cabling a new studio.

A few weeks after beginning at TVW an Outside Broadcast (OB) was planned at the airport. Extra crew were needed to run cables, set up scaffolding and carry equipment.

It was great! As well as a considerable amount of overtime, it meant getting out of the maintenance area and into fresh air!

After that I was always first to volunteer for any Outside Broadcasts!

I spent as much time as possible in the OB area but occasionally I was roped into helping out in the studio. One day I was asked to operate the boom microphone during a local afternoon show.

After a brief description of how it worked, I was left to it.

At one point there was a difficult manoeuvre where the back end of the boom was likely to knock over part of the set!

While I was watching the back end of the boom, the microphone at the other end snagged the netting on a lady's hat and whipped it off her head!

"

The microphone ... snagged the netting on a lady's hat and whipped it off her head!

When I turned back, the compère, Lloyd Lawson, was chasing after the boom to retrieve the hat!

Later I apologised to the producer/director. She said it was the best thing that had happened on the show for a long time!

When TVW decided to cover WAFL football matches I became a full-time member of OBs.

We covered the matches with two cameras at the back of the grandstand. One close-up camera and one wide-shot camera. For finals and interstate matches we had a third camera placed on the boundary.

There were no facilities for supers, to allow us to superimpose the score, so when a goal was scored we would switch between the close-up camera showing the scoreboard and the wide shot following the ball. During the week we would move links, camera platforms and various other pieces of equipment to the next ground and run cables.

After the football season ended there was very little work in OBs, so I was rostered into Audio.

I was given a brief training period and then let loose on the afternoon Kids' show!

After a few years in OBs and Audio, I was asked to fill in as Master Control Operator during the day.

There was no computerised switching system or remote controls in those days.

It was all manual!

Telecine and videotapes were rolled manually after a cue over the Talkback System. Videotape machines took between four and eight seconds to lock up and stabilise, so they required a ten-second pre-roll!

The only aid for program switching was a ten-second Countdown Generator triggered by cues recorded on all films and videotapes.

During the day there were always a number of cheap commercials consisting of a few slides and a voice-over announcement.

The voice-over was mostly live from an Announce Booth. The whole time the Station was on air someone was rostered to sit in the Announce Booth. A book of scripts would be supplied to the Booth, Audio and Master Control.

A few voice-over announcements came from vinyl records at either 78 rpm or 45 rpm. At that time it was felt that viewers may not be able to distinguish between the end of one commercial and the start of the next so a starburst was used to separate them!

The starburst came from film and lasted two seconds. A typical sequence of slide and voice-over commercial followed by videotape and separated with a starburst might be as follows:

- Master Control Switcher: Take Telecine (slide)
- Talkback to Telecine: "change slide"
- Talkback to Telecine: "change slide"
- Talkback to Videotape: "roll tape" (10 sec. pre-roll)
- Talkback to Telecine: "change slide"
- Talkback to Telecine: "roll film" (5 sec. pre-roll)
- Master Control Switcher: Take film (starburst)
- Master Control Switcher: Take videotape

One of the best master control operators was also a practical joker.

One night when an On Air program was being switched by a director from Studio 2 control rooms, he patched the studio 2 "OFF AIR" monitor to an Auxiliary Switcher in Master Control. He then switched random vision sources on the auxiliary switcher.

The director thought that the spurious vision he could see on his "OFF AIR" monitor was going to air!

Meanwhile the correct vision was going to air from the master control switcher!

I hope the director had a good sense of humour!

TVW had a strict dress code. Sneakers, jeans and T-shirts were not allowed. Normal shoes, trousers, shirt and tie were required by all male staff including floor crew. Technicians and workshop staff generally wore overalls.

Like the police and military forces at the time, a neat moustache was acceptable but a beard was not!

All women (except On Air staff) wore a uniform consisting of a dark blue skirt and light blue blouse.

However, there was one person who was not familiar with the strict dress rules: Tom Creamer!

Tom came to Australia from England under a Migrant scheme to work at TVW.

He was sent to work on Outside Broadcasts! A real "learning experience"!

At the time we were running cables at Ascot Racecourse in preparation for the Perth Cup held on New Year's Day.

The temperature was in the high thirties and humidity was high due to watering the track. We told Tom to take it easy but he insisted on doing his share!

By the end of the day Tom was very red in the face, which was definitely not helped by his thick bushy beard!

A few days later Tom turned up at work minus the beard.

Someone must have told him of the Station policy on beards.

He told me later that he had been married for ten years and his wife had never seen him without a beard!

WASHED OUT

Once a year, TVW televised an Open Day event at the Castledare Boys Home in a bid to raise money for the home.

The day before, we would run cables and rig links. A Link consists of a transmitter and receiver used to transmit video and audio signals more than 100 kilometres. The signal is focussed in a narrow beam and requires a clear line of sight to the receiver.

The kids were great! They would help us run cables. As many as five or six of them would join forces and run a camera cable.

Years later I heard that some of the boys were abused. Not a happy place!

The link path required a "double hop" to reach TVW studios. The first link hop was from Castledare to the State Government Office building. The repeater site was on the top floor of the building located in West Perth, opposite the entrance to King's Park. We de-rigged the links the day after the OB.

That particular day happened to be a public holiday and the building was deserted except for a kiosk for tourists on the top floor.

I was stacking equipment in the back of a small support truck when the truck started to shake violently. Thinking someone on the outside was rocking the truck, I got out to check and found the ground was shaking. The outside of the bottom floor of the building was a sheet of eight-foot-high glass the full length of the building.

Waves were running through the glass!

At that moment the two other members of the crew rushed out of the lift and ran out of the building. The lady in the kiosk was the only one left in the building.

When the shaking stopped, we went back to see if she was OK. She was.

It was the Meckering Earthquake, October 14, 1968. Fortunately there were no fatalities or serious injuries, but there was structural damage to buildings and roads, with extensive damage to the town of Meckering where most buildings were either destroyed or badly damaged.

One very different, but certainly interesting, Outside Broadcast, was the official opening of the Mount Newman Mine. The idea was to simultaneously show the opening in London, Paris, New York and Tokyo. At that time the only uplink to a satellite was from Parkes in NSW.

A fast jet was hired to fly a videotape of the opening from Mount Newman to the nearest airfield to Parkes.

Preparations underway for the coverage of the Mount Newman Mine opening

The satellite at that time could only handle TV signals in the American 525 line 60 Hz system not our 625 line 50 Hz system. We had to change all our equipment to the American system including Sync Pulse Generator (SPG), TR3 and TR5 videotape machines, and cameras.

> "When I reached forward to attach a microphone on the director, one of the cheetahs smacked my hand away with its paw …

Another problem was that the opening was early in the week and we were covering the football on Saturday. Not enough time to drive the OB van from Perth to Mount Newman!

We hired a truck and fitted it out with the TR3 and TR5 tape machines and some other basic equipment. However, the cameras and some other items were needed for the football. The hire truck left Perth in plenty of time to drive to Mount Newman.

After the football I packed up the cameras and other equipment and took them to the airport, where I loaded them onto an aircraft and flew to Mount Newman with them.

To power the hired OB van we used a 60 Hz generator to match the American TV system. The TR3 tape machine didn't like that, so we had to power the TR3 with a separate 50 Hz generator!

After the successful telecast of the Mount Newman Mine Opening, attention turned to our smallest OB van … the International Harvester van!

The van was upgraded with a transistorised Bosch camera. The camera came with a 14-to-1 zoom lens with electronic (servo) controls. Our other zoom lenses had manual controls.

To test the International Harvester van, it was sent to the Perth Zoo where we were to interview the newly-appointed zoo director.

The director had two pet cheetahs!

He said he used to walk the cheetahs on a lead, taking them through the streets in Scotland. Many people just thought they were dogs!

We set up a suitable spot for an interview, with the two cheetahs sitting on either side of the director.

When I reached forward to attach a microphone on the director, one of the cheetahs smacked my hand away with its paw and glared at me.

It was being protective!

I wasn't about to challenge it, so I handed the microphone to the director and explained how to put it on.

The worst OB that I ever worked on was car racing at Wanneroo. Wanneroo is about an hour's drive north of Perth and the track is a few kilometres in from the coast. The track was straddled over the top of a hill with very few trees for shelter. A few days before the OB a strong low-pressure system established itself just off the coast, with gale force winds and driving non-stop rain.

The link path was a double hop from Wanneroo to our Station Transmitter tower at Bickley then from Bickley to TVW studios.

Microwave link at TVW's Bickley Tower

We set up the links on the Station Transmitter tower a few days previously when the weather was OK. Lining up the second hop and setting up the receiver for the first hop from Wanneroo. The receiver was lined up approximately by sight.

The crew was rostered to rig the OB the day before. The camera cables were thick multicore cables with high voltages and came in 100 foot and 200 foot lengths. For long cable runs several cables had to be joined end to end. The joins had to be kept perfectly dry. They were wrapped in plastic and kept above ground with wooden stakes.

While the crew were running cables I set up the Link Transmitter. The link transmitter's microwave signal is focussed in a narrow beam by a four foot diameter dish. The dish is panned and tilted for maximum signal level in the receiver at Bickley. A tech at Bickley relays signal level information by VHF radio.

With gale force winds and driving rain it was very difficult. After numerous attempts the signal level was still not good enough. The Link Receiver at Bickley must have been off line. Someone would have to climb the Station Transmitter tower at Bickley to adjust the Link Receiver Dish.

Nobody was going to volunteer in this storm so the chief engineer, John Quicke, did it.

Master Control said the video signal was useable.

Rigging was going to be a full day's work under normal conditions. Under these atrocious conditions we were still going in the dark using vehicles' headlights to see. When we finally finished we got in the vehicles and headed for the exit, only to find the exit gates closed and padlocked.

With no mobile phones in those days, we called Master Control on VHF radio. Fortunately they were still listening to the radio. I gave the master control operator the contact number for the car racing. About an hour later the track caretaker arrived to unlock the gates.

Another hour's drive back to the Station. Then we unloaded empty cable drums and loaded cameras, lenses, tripod and other gear for the following day.

After picking up a hamburger along the way I arrived home at about 11 pm completely exhausted. We were due to start the following morning at 6 am. I set the alarm for 5 am.

The next thing I remember was the phone ringing. Peter said, "Why aren't you here at work? You should have been here fifteen minutes ago." Either I slept through the alarm or I turned it off in my sleep.

I asked Peter to take the crew and the support vehicles, drive to the racing track and start setting up cameras. I was the only one on the crew with a licence to drive the OB van. After throwing on some clothes I raced in to the Station, then headed for Wanneroo in the OB van.

It was still very windy and raining steadily. The cameras had to be kept covered with tarps at all times. Once the generator was started and the OB van switched on, we started switching on cameras. But one of the cameras wasn't working!

We kept a spare set of modules in the van but they didn't help. There was water in the frame wiring, causing a short!

We had a spare camera frame at the studios. I called Master Control and asked to have the spare frame sent to us.

Being a weekend there was nobody spare at the Station. So once again it fell to the chief engineer to pick up the spare frame and head for Wanneroo.

The last few kilometres from the main road to the track were unsealed. A passing petrol-head spun his wheels, sending rocks flying and breaking Quickey's windscreen. He was not happy!

By the end of the race the rain had stopped and the sun was shining.

The following Monday I was called to Quickey's office. He had found out I was late for work and was not impressed. I wonder who told him?

THE NEW VAN

My working experiences went from over-protective cheetahs, to "bigger is better" when Management decided we needed a new Outside Broadcast van.

Brian Treasure said anything from Western Australia should be as big as or bigger than anything in the Eastern States!

The biggest OB van in Australia at the time was ATV 0's van (ATV 0 later became ATV 10). ATV 0 belonged to Reg Ansett, Australia's richest man at that time. So ATV was one of the newest and best-equipped stations in Australia.

Their OB van was a semi-trailer van based on American vans at the time. American vans owned by the major networks were designed to be self-contained with an on-board power generator and storage for cameras, cables and other equipment. They could travel interstate at a moment's notice.

The bodywork and major infrastructure of TVW's new van was built by Ansair, an Ansett company which built ATV's van. The TVW van was the same as ATV's except for the rack layout inside.

The installation was subcontracted to Broadcast Engineering. Vic Kitney and I were sent to Melbourne to install equipment and cables. For the installation the van was located in one corner of a warehouse in South Melbourne.

The work was supervised by Howard Jones from Broadcast Engineering. Vic and I had considerable input to the job. We were assisted by an apprentice from Astor. Philips owned Astor at the time.

On my first day off I went looking for a car. If we were going to be stuck in Melbourne for a number of weeks I wanted a car. I bought a cheap old Holden station wagon. In our days off we toured around a great deal of Victoria.

One day Vic and I went to ATV 0 to have a look at their OB van. We met their OB supervisor, Frank Verstrepen. Frank was working at TVW as an audio operator when I first joined TVW but he left soon after. I was told that he went to work on a pirate radio station in the North Sea!

Another day, we were working in our OB van listening to the radio when we heard a news report that a section of the Westgate Bridge had collapsed while under construction. We turned on the off-air monitor and switched between channels. ATV was first with live pictures. Thirty-five workers were killed and a Royal Commission was set up to investigate the cause.

Installation of equipment in the new van

Collapse of Westgate Bridge under construction

Eventually, we finished the van's installation, including three 4½ inch Image Orthicon cameras. A Philips Engineer, Hassell Bart, then installed two LDK 3 colour cameras. A third colour camera (of an earlier vintage) from HSV 7 was also installed in the van.

This was October, 1970, four years before the introduction of colour TV into Australia.

An invitation had been sent to other TV stations to look at the van which was complete with colour cameras. For this purpose we parked the van outside the Philips building in South Melbourne.

When we started the generator the voltage became erratic and couldn't be used, so we called in an electrician to run a three phase power feed from the building.

The next day Chief Engineer John Quicke and Vic drove the van to Adelaide, while I followed in my car.

The company which manufactured the faulty diesel generator was located in Adelaide, so we went to their factory. They disconnected the generator, lifted it out with a forklift, replaced it with a new one, then connected and tested it.

We headed for Port Augusta in the OB van and Holden station wagon to load the OB van on to a train.

Then John Quicke, Vic and I drove to Perth in the station wagon, taking turns in driving.

From Ceduna to the border the going was pretty rugged! The road wasn't sealed on the South Australian side.

When the new OB van arrived at the Station everyone wanted to see it in operation!

Engineer Hassell Bart installing Philips cameras

OB van outside Philips Building

OB van loaded on train at Port Augusta

TVW OB vehicles

We parked the van in the back car park and started the diesel generator. This time the generator's frequency was erratic and couldn't be used. The first two times we tried to use the generator it had failed. Not a good record of reliability!

Except for a trial run at Gloucester Park Trotting Track, the first OB for the new van was a cricket Test Match against England at the WACA. That was the first-ever Test Match held in Perth!

The new OB van wouldn't fit inside the ground so a new parking bay had to be constructed on the south side of the oval.

We still had the three colour cameras in the van. A large scaffold was built with three platform levels: one for commentators, one for black and white cameras and one for colour cameras. Colour pictures were linked back to the Station to be watched in colour in the boardroom. The colour burst was stripped off the signal for transmission off air. Hassell Bart was Technical Director for the colour cameras.

After the cricket, the three colour cameras were returned to Philips and HSV Channel 7 in Melbourne and our new OB van was reduced to three black and white cameras. The next major Outside Broadcast was the Miss West Coast final at Beatty Park. The OB was rigged on Friday (all cables run, links set up and checked and cameras set up and checked), then rehearsals the next day, and the final program live to air Saturday night.

It was late Friday afternoon before we had the cameras set up ready to look at pictures. We switched on the cameras. Cameras 1 and 3 looked good but Camera 2's picture was rolling as if it was not synchronised. I was checking the pulse signals to the camera when Les the audio operator told me that the Audio Equaliser was not working and could I fix it?

Finding the problem with the camera was a higher priority, so I asked if it was really necessary. The audio equaliser was installed in the van when the van was in Melbourne and put on show at the Philips building. The equaliser did not belong to us. It was on loan for appearances.

> Two wires on the extender had been swapped over! It had cost me hours of work!

Then I was told that all of the voice-over announcements and background music had been pre-recorded and edited, then transferred to a master tape. Some of it was Tenth Generation recording (really!). Now Les was trying to compensate for the loss of high frequency component.

I told Les I didn't have time to look at the equaliser and thought it was a bit late to be trying to correct the frequency response.

The problem with the camera would need a CRO (Cathode Ray Oscilloscope) to track down the cause so I called the station and asked for a CRO to be sent out.

While I waited I dug out a "box of tricks" that came with the cameras and found a service manual and module extenders. They were brand new, wrapped in plastic. I had never looked at the circuit boards or circuit diagrams.

It was all new!

I selected the module which seemed to be the most likely to be the problem and put it on the module extender. When I turned the power back on, the fault was even worse!

I spent the next hour tracing signals around the board but seemed to be going around in circles. The rest of the crew had finished for the day and returned to the station. The security guards checked in, so I showed them what had to be watched.

The fault in the camera appeared to originate in the camera head. That meant moving the CRO inside the building. Tracing signals through the head unit led back to the CCU in the OB van. Each time I put the module on the module extender it caused the fault to change so I started checking around the module extender.

Two wires on the extender had been swapped over!

It had cost me hours of work!

A new extender still in its plastic wrapping?

After correcting the extender wiring, the camera still had the original fault. But now I was familiar with many of the circuits. It didn't take very long to track down the fault and fix it. I clocked off at 2100.

On Saturday I started before the rest of the crew, to switch on the van, cameras and links. Once the production crew arrived and began rehearsals there wasn't much for me to do but keep an eye on everything and make some minor adjustments.

I found our audio operator, Les, had removed the audio equaliser from the racks, sent it back to the Station, had someone fix it and returned it to the OB van racks. Les had no experience or knowledge of the wiring behind the racks and could have caused serious problems.

Then I was told he didn't use the equaliser. I was not happy and let him know it!

On Monday I had a visit from Max Bostock in the OB garage.

Max asked if I had refused to help Audio fix some equipment they needed for the show. I replied that I had a major problem with a camera and thought that was a higher priority than a new toy they wanted to play with!

Max said he had been told it was an essential piece of equipment. I said, "Why didn't they use it when it was fixed and returned ready for use?"

Max had been told that they didn't want to use the equaliser on the show because it wasn't available for rehearsals. I told him I didn't believe that was the reason and explained how multiple generations of recording onto a master tape would result in a significant loss of high frequencies. Using the equaliser to recover the high frequencies would result in an increase in noise.

"

An on-board generator sounds good in theory but in practice it was a waste of space!

Max agreed the sound quality was not good but the program was successful.

After Miss West Coast, things went fairly quiet. Time to evaluate.

An on-board generator sounds good in theory but in practice it was a waste of space!

Its reliability was a problem, so for major OBs we would always arrange Mains power from the State Electricity Commission.

Double springing and a heavy lined sound-proof compartment reduced sound and vibration but did not eliminate it. Exhaust fumes would often get sucked into the air-conditioning intake. An exhaust duct strapped to the roof of the van sometimes helped divert it.

"I could feel a change was about to happen!"

The generator was eventually removed from the van and installed in a separate vehicle. The generator could be parked some distance downwind from the van.

No vibration, no noise and no fumes!

The on-board storage of cameras and cables also sounds good but in practice it, too, was a waste of space.

We would normally pre-rig major OBs so the cables would be removed from the van and taken to the site by tender truck. The reverse would happen in de-rigging Mostly the cables were only stored in the OB van when it was parked in the garage.

The van's facilities were put to good use in the city when Perth City Council was having a very public argument with its Town Planner.

The City Council called a Special Meeting to discuss the matter and the OB van was sent to cover the meeting. I was driving the OB van down Pier Street in the city, on the way to the council building when the OB van brakes locked up!

I had just pulled out to pass a parked car when it happened, so the van was blocking both lanes. It was late afternoon and just building up to peak-hour traffic. I called Master Control on the radio and asked them to call our station mechanic, Darcy Bisot, and ask his advice.

After about half an hour John Quicke turned up in another prime mover. After changing prime movers the brakes released and the van moved off. Our prime mover had a leak in the air line for the air brakes ... that was the cause of the problem!

In June, 1971, the International Harvester van and its trailer-mounted diesel generator was sent to Port Augusta by train. I also travelled to Port Augusta by train and picked up the van there. I was to deliver the van and generator to SAS Channel 10 in Adelaide.

I could feel a change was about to happen!

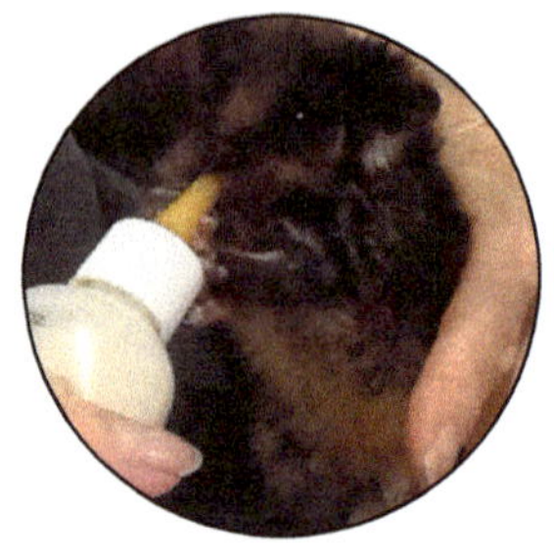

A NEW LIFE

In June, 1971, I was the Outside Broadcast Supervisor for TVW Channel 7, responsible for the OB garage and four vehicles. Although I had a feeling a change was coming … in reality I had no idea what was about to change!

In Perth, the largest of the vehicles was a semi-trailer OB van with three 4½ inch PYE Image Orthicon cameras, a TR60 videotape machine and an on-board diesel generator.

The next largest vehicle was an Austin OB van with three 4½ inch PYE IO cameras.

Then there was an International Harvester 4WD vehicle with one Bosch 3 inch IO camera and a TR5 videotape machine.

We also had a diesel generator on a trailer. It was often towed by the International Harvester van. These OB vans were backed up by a support truck.

I was thirty years old and I had been working for TVW for seven years when they sent me to Adelaide with the International Harvester OB van.

Back to Port Augusta again!

The train trip from Perth to Port Augusta was pleasant, but then I had to drive the OB van with the generator trailer from Port Augusta to Adelaide.

I had been pushing the van and generator fairly hard and the motor was getting hot, so I pulled into a service station at Port Wakefield.

I was checking the water level in the radiator when a car towing a trailer full of building materials stopped alongside of me. The driver got out of the car and said, "Hi, I'm Kevin Earle. I work for Channel 10."

Kevin told me he was heading for Moonta to work on his holiday house. The family were with him, waiting in the car. He was very friendly and offered to help in any way he could.

I had a good description of how to get to SAS Channel 10 in Adelaide and Kevin confirmed the information was correct.

I found SAS fairly easily. As the car park was nearly full, I continued down the driveway towards the rear of the building. One of the floor crew greeted me and said they were expecting me. They had made room for the van to park in the Props area. After parking the van and locking it, I was shown the way upstairs to the Studio Control Room. Max Bostock was there and he introduced me to several people.

In the Studio they were playing TV Bingo and through the glass window I could see rows of seats with people playing the game. Two women were moving up and down the aisles between the seats handing out cards. Max suggested we go to our apartment and get settled in. The apartment was in a multi-storeyed building in North Adelaide, with views of Adelaide and Mount Lofty. There were three separate bedrooms allocated to Max, Terry Willesee and me.

After I unpacked, Max explained the situation at SAS. He said I was to show the local technicians and production staff how to operate the OB vehicle.

It was an open-ended arrangement. I was to stay in Adelaide for as long as necessary. It was getting late when Max said some of the SAS staff were heading into the city to a restaurant for dinner and we were invited. The restaurant was the BBQ Inn, located in Hindley Street, one of the less desirable parts of the city. A large table had been organised and people were starting to be seated.

I found myself seated next to a very attractive woman who was introduced as Margie Taylor, Publicity Manager. I recognised her as one of the women handing out bingo cards on the studio floor. She was very friendly and easy to talk to.

“ I found myself seated next to a very attractive woman who was introduced as Margie Taylor ...

During the meal it was mentioned a woman who worked at SAS was having a party at her flat in a couple of days. Max asked if I wanted to go, so I said yes, since I had nothing else to do and nowhere to go. When we arrived at the party it was very crowded for a small flat, and I didn't know anyone. Then

Margie walked in. We had a drink together, but the music was so loud it was difficult to talk. It had been a long day and I was feeling tired but didn't know how to get back to the apartment.

I said, "Do you think they would let me make a phone call for a taxi?" (No mobile phones then.)

Margie said, "I can give you a lift."

"

Attractive. Intelligent. Single. Drives an MG. Got to be my lucky day.

"Are you sure? I don't want to take you out of your way."

"It's no trouble."

We left the party and started walking down the street past several cars. I wondered which car was hers. She stopped alongside a white MG Midget. "Hop in," she said. Must come from a rich family I thought!

On the way back to the apartment Margie asked if I would like to see some of Adelaide the following day. I said that I would love to, if I wasn't taking her away from family or work. She said there was only her mum and a dog and a cat.

Attractive. Intelligent. Single. Drives an MG. Got to be my lucky day. The next day we drove along all the beaches. Had lunch along the way and arranged to catch up the following week.

One thing led to another in the next few weeks and we spent every available minute together. A lot of time was spent at Margie's home which she shared with her mum. I also met her dog, Tuffey, and cat, Flick. Often Margie's GP, Than Singh, would call by. He had a great sense of humour and became a good friend. We made a couple of trips to the Adelaide Hills. It fascinated me that the Hills were so close to the city, unlike in Perth.

> “We had been talking about living together and it seemed logical and desirable to get married.

Most of the SAS staff were friendly and often organised social events. One group arranged horse-riding on weekends. I had been horse riding in Perth a couple of times, but Margie and I were both learners and it was fun.

After a couple of months, I was aware I would soon be recalled to Perth. I didn’t want to go. Margie felt the same way. Either I could shift to Adelaide or Margie could shift to Perth.

It seemed to me it would be better if I moved to Adelaide.

We had been talking about living together and it seemed logical and desirable to get married. I knew that waiting another three to six months wouldn’t change anything. Margie agreed and so we set about making plans for our future.

We decided to keep our plans secret except for a few people. First we told Margie’s mum and my parents. Then we bought an engagement ring.

I had to tell Max, to find out if I could move to Adelaide permanently. Max said he thought it could be handled as an internal company transfer. I asked Than if he would be best man and he said he would be delighted.

To organise a honeymoon we had to book holidays at the same time. Max helped to arrange that. Margie had been to Magnetic Island before and suggested we both go there. She gave me details of a travel agent and I made the necessary arrangements. Margie arranged a party for the night we were married. We would leave for Magnetic Island the next morning. At the party the Channel's newsreader, Terry Willesee (also from Perth), noticed the rings Margie was wearing and the real reason for the party was revealed.

> ”
> We began looking at properties in the Hills. We wanted a house with a few acres of land.

The Honeymoon was perfect and so was the weather. We met Charlie the pineapple farmer and old friend of Margie's.

Unfortunately I picked up a throat infection on the last day.

The next day we were due back at work but I was going to call in sick.

Margie said we should face the music together so I put in an appearance at work then went home sick. Than looked at my throat and said I had Quinsy Tonsillitis. He gave me a shot of penicillin and told me to take the week off!

We moved into a flat on East Terrace. It was comfortable and convenient. Only a short drive to the Station. With parklands just across the road it was good for walking with Tuffey. My car arrived from Perth along with my stereo sound system and clothes. There were restaurants and shops nearby. We were well set up and very happy with life all round.

As much as we enjoyed living on East Terrace we wanted to have our own home. We both wanted to live in either the Hills or near the beach. I had lived near the beach and didn't find it much different to the suburbs. I would prefer the open spaces of the Hills and Margie agreed.

I asked my parents to sell the house I had in Perth. It meant they would have to move into their unit in Scarborough. We began looking at properties in the Hills. We wanted a house with a few acres of land. One looked fairly promising, with a small modern house on about two acres.

Then a real estate agent, Pat Coffey, told us about an old house with ten acres of land. It had been for sale for some time and the owners had reduced the price several times. He suggested they might drop the price another $1,500.

Inspection was by appointment only. When Pat showed us the property Margie said she remembered going past the place as a child and was very keen to buy it. The house was a very old building with several old sheds and stables. But it was good value if they accepted our offer. The offer was on condition that we could sell the house in Perth.

We had a couple of stressful weeks, waiting for the sale of the Perth property. On the last day the Perth sale went through! We had arranged for a loan of $5,000 to cover the difference and moving costs.

Moving in on February 25th, 1972, was a great relief!

A horse called Merrylegs had been living on the property and was allowed to continue. We met our neighbours, Max and Audrey Pollock and Max's parents, Nanna and Poppa Pollock, and became good friends.

Poppa Pollock was in his nineties. He told us that when he was a small boy the Adelaide to Melbourne Stagecoach would come down our road and change horses at the bottom of the road!

Tuffey and Flick moved in and seemed to like the place. Weekend BBQs and working bees became a regular event. Our next additions to the animal population were two horses. They would be followed by donkeys and goats.

"
Our next additions to the animal population were two horses. They would be followed by donkeys and goats.

A kangaroo was advertised for sale. We didn't know the best way to transport a kangaroo but decided to use a closed-in horse float. Kevin Earle offered to provide a car with a towbar for the purpose. Kevin and family had become good friends. We would often play cards, either at our home or theirs, we stayed at their holiday house at Moonta and they often spent Christmas Eve at our place.

Our kangaroo was kept in a round yard originally designed for training horses.

Margie soon found out how dangerous an adult female kangaroo can be!

She went into the yard to feed the kangaroo but it stood up on its hind legs and tail and lashed out with the claw in its hind legs ripping Margie's jeans…and more!

One day I saw an eagle dive into a tree then fly off with a possum in its claws. I went to the tree to investigate and saw a nest high up. Something seemed to be moving, so I climbed the tree and found a baby ringtail possum clinging to the nest.

I collected the baby possum and brought it back to the house. Margie was pleased and soon learnt how to hand-rear a possum! She named it Pyewacket.

We had firmly established ourselves in our House and Property.

The property we had just bought was covered with blackberry bushes. About one third of the paddocks consisted of bushes six to eight feet high!

The berries are good to eat but the bushes are classed as noxious weeds! They grow and spread rapidly and birds and foxes spread the seeds to neighbouring properties.

So I bought a knapsack spray kit and poison spray. Lugging a knapsack full of spray around a paddock was not much fun and very slow going. I complained about this to our neighbour Max.

Max grinned and gave a "nudge, nudge, wink, wink" look and said, "Follow me." He had a shed and workshop down by his dam. When we got there he pointed to a tractor in the shed. It was an old tractor but obviously well kept.

Mounted on the back of the tractor was a forty-four-gallon drum. Next to the forty-four-gallon drum was a pump, powered by the tractor; fitted to the pump was a hand spray nozzle on a ten-metre-long pressure hose.

Max said I could borrow it but not to drive it on the road as it wasn't registered.

I had a driver's licence to cover anything from a bike to a semi-trailer – but Max's tractor was a new experience.

In one day I emptied the forty-four-gallon drum ten times!

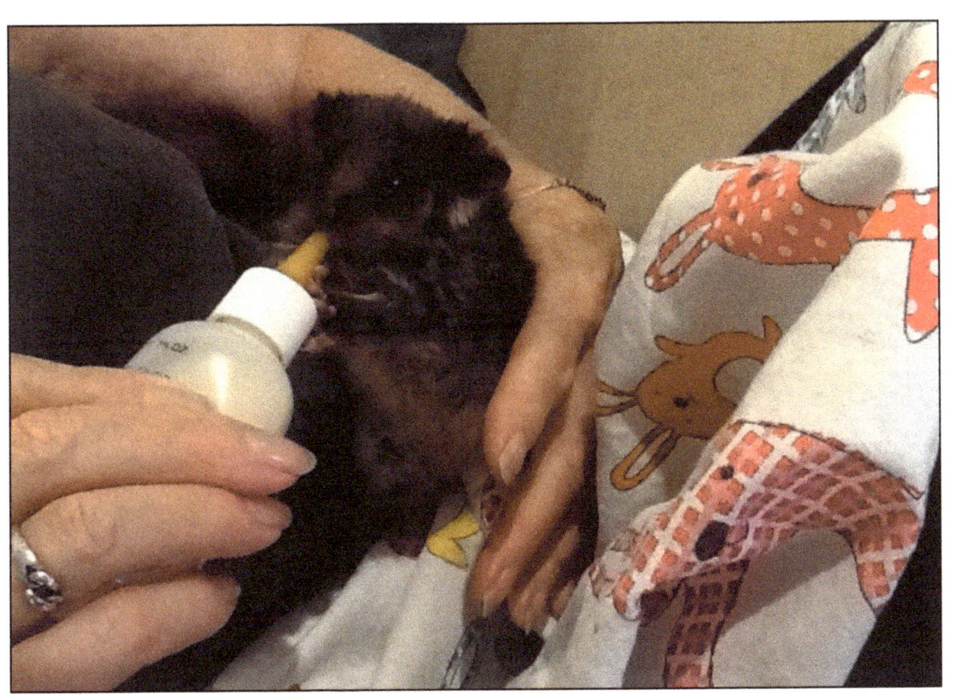

Bottle feeding Pyewacket

Linus sees the berry pickers

When I finished using the tractor, I thought I should return it in good condition. When checking the tyre pressures I found the back tyres had some water in them.

I asked Max if he knew about the water and he told me the back tyres were half full of water to keep the centre of gravity down low on the steep hills.

The blackberry bushes soon died off, leaving clumps of dead brambles with a new set of seedlings sprouting up. Each year they reduced until one knapsack covered the whole property.

Most farmers object to strangers pushing down fences to help themselves to the blackberries. They pick only the best and most accessible berries.

One day I saw a group of berry pickers in the far corner of our property so I got into the car and drove around the road to where they were. I told them that the blackberry bushes had just been sprayed with poison.

They weren't happy berry pickers!

We shared our northern boundary fence with neighbours, who bought the property as an investment. They didn't want to spend any money on it and didn't care if our animals strayed onto it.

Weeds hadn't been sprayed and some huge blackberry bushes had thrived for years. The best ones were more than a hundred metres from the main road.

One group of berry pickers decided it was worth the effort, and they had been picking for some time when Linus spotted them.

Linus was a very curious, very determined little donkey … he was also very greedy!

Whenever I was working in the paddock he would come to see what I was doing. If I bent down to pull out a weed, Linus would rest his head on my shoulder.

When Linus saw the berry pickers he had to find out what they were doing.

Before anyone knew what had happened, Linus knocked over a couple of containers of berries. He ate some and then started to check what each person was doing. The berry pickers decided they had had enough, fending off the pushy donkey.

They picked up everything they could recover and hurried back to their car with Linus in hot pursuit!

Max liked a few cold beers on a hot day and often brewed his own home brew. He also made a very good blackberry wine and he kept a few good blackberry bushes near his dam for that very reason.

After killing off all the bushes on our place we were left with big clumps of dead bushes to burn.

In February, 1983, the Ash Wednesday bushfire swept through our place and Max's property, burning all the blackberries – along with considerable damage to our place and to those around us.

Unfortunately, sadly, it also destroyed Max's tractor!

COLOUR

The International Harvester van was soon put to work recording commercials, no other Station in Adelaide had this sort of facility.

One of the first jobs for the van was to cover the Moratorium March, a protest against the Vietnam War.

The van and generator joined in the march with the camera on the roof of the van. TVW News Editor Darcy Farrell walked alongside the van, giving commentary and interviewing protesters. Tapes were sent back to the studio by taxi and put to air. Even though there was a short delay it gave the appearance of being live to air.

SAS Channel 10 started out with a News Department but when it ran into financial problems the Newsroom had to go. The Australian Journalist Association was not happy with this but as long as SAS had financial problems they couldn't do much about it. When TVW acquired SAS, the AJA applied pressure to restore the SAS Newsroom. They said TVW could afford it.

Managing Director James Cruthers (later to become Sir James) commented that as Adelaide already had three news programs (Channel 9 and 7 and the ABC), why should SAS produce a fourth?

However TVW had already planned to produce a news service as well as develop OB facilities.

When SAS closed the Newsroom some of the hardware was kept.

The car two-way radios were stacked in a cupboard.

One of the radios was immediately installed in the International Harvester van.

One of the first times the van was called for by the Newsroom was a report that an entire family had been murdered. It happened in an isolated farmhouse in the Adelaide Hills. Details about the location of the farmhouse were vague.

The Newsroom suggested I take the van to Willunga and wait for further directions. I had just arrived at Willunga when the Newsroom called with instructions to drive along the Willunga to Meadows road. After several conflicting directions I saw several vehicles parked around a farmhouse about 200 metres from the main road.

It was the right one!

I parked next to the SAS News car and set up the camera on the roof of the van. The video camera and videotape recorder had the advantage in that it could be replayed immediately.

A film camera would need to have the film developed. However the news cameraman, Mark Hall, said he preferred to use the film camera because it was more portable.

I left the video camera set up as a backup. Police had confirmed that ten bodies had been found in the house. Seven were children. They began to bring out the bodies. Each body was on a stretcher, covered with a sheet.

” All we needed was an event to cover!

An arm had dropped over the side of one stretcher. It was a child. The skin was white and shiny, turning blue.

There was complete silence. It seemed unreal.

I wanted to stop it, turn back time and have a different ending.

There was nothing anyone could do now. We all just watched in silence. I packed up the camera and returned to the Station.

One day, months later, returning from a trip to Victor Harbour via Meadows, I recognised the section from Willunga to Meadows and the turnoff to the farmhouse. But the farmhouse was gone. No sign that it had ever existed. No souvenirs for anyone to take, but I can still see children's bodies on stretchers!

Clifford Cecil Bartholomew thought his wife was having an affair so he shot his wife and his seven children, as well as two relatives who had the misfortune of being there at the time.

In less than twelve months TVW's old Austin OB van was sent to SAS with the three 3 inch IO (Image Orthicon) cameras replaced with three 4½ inch IO cameras. We now had a three-camera van and a single-camera van to work with.

All we needed was an event to cover!

At the time, South Australia was leading in the Sheffield Shield cricket. They only had to draw against Victoria to win the

Shield, but Victoria was out of the running, so no Victorian TV station was interested in covering the match.

A crew from SAS drove the Austin OB van to Melbourne and set up cameras at the MCG. We set up a link from the MCG to the Telecom building and patched into the bearer system to cover the match live to Adelaide.

"

In an effort to raise SAS 10's profile in Adelaide we began covering soccer, baseball, greyhound racing and any other event of public interest!

In an effort to raise SAS 10's profile in Adelaide we began covering soccer, baseball, greyhound racing and any other event of public interest.

Max told me to drive the van around the streets of Adelaide if I had nothing else to do. Like a travelling Billboard.

In 1972 and 1973 we did more than 110 major OBs per year, as well as 70 commercials and other smaller jobs. Then Harry Kelly arrived from TVW to tell us that all productions had to be costed and make a profit. Publicity, promotion and raising the Station's profile didn't count for anything!

We went from 110 OBs in 1973 to 26 in 1974.

One day Max called me into the boardroom to tell me he believed new technology was causing rapid changes in OBs. He talked about a VW Kombi van which was used as a three camera van.

Then he suggested that Fibre Optics would make Microwave Links obsolete. We could just plug into the nearest Fibre Optic like a telephone. The next day I decided to see Max and debate some of his ideas. But he had returned to Perth.

A few months later I was working on an OB when someone told me that our newly appointed Director of Engineering, Peter Smith, had bought a vehicle to be used as a colour OB van.

I couldn't believe it, but when I returned to the Station the van was standing in the car park. It was a Mercedes camper van.

It was pathetic! It was even smaller than the Austin van!

Peter Smith had never been on an OB in his life, and the only person he appeared to have consulted had also never been on an OB.

I had the feeling that Max had got to him. I had several heated arguments with Peter about the size of the van. I said that there was just enough room for three cameras but no room for any additional equipment.

He said, "There will never be more than three cameras on an OB in Adelaide."

I said there was no room for any spare parts or test equipment. He said, "Think of an OB as being an aeroplane – once you're in the air it's too late to do any maintenance."

I tried to make the best use of the room I had, unlike the waste of space in the semi-trailer van. The rack frame ran lengthwise down the Mercedes van and curved slightly to follow the shape of the van. Also, the rack frame was on wheels, so it could be wound out for rear access to equipment. Two air conditioners were mounted on the roof. It looked strange and made the vehicle top heavy but there was nowhere else to put them.

One tech said, "You don't need that much air conditioning. I've got one at home that puts out X cubic metres per minute of cold air in a room with a volume of Y cubic metres. It should take Y divided by X minutes to cool down."

So I said, "You're talking about an insulated box. I'm talking about a metal box standing in the sun, filled with a few tons of equipment acting as a heat sink, and four or five people, all generating kilowatts of heat."

Then I said, "I have been told not to think of air conditioning like a sausage machine. Feed in cold air one end and extract hot air the other end. Instead of replacing the air, the air mixes to halve the temperature difference."

The debate was referred to Peter Smith and the resulting compromise was inefficient.

After a lot of hard work, we had the Mercedes OB van ready for the annual Christmas Pageant. Colour TV was due to begin in 1975, but a few months before this, we were told live Outside Broadcasts in colour would be permitted as a test.

On November 9, 1974, we televised the John Martin's Christmas Pageant in colour. I believe this was the first colour program in South Australia and possibly the first in Australia. Building a colour OB van created a lot of new problems which kept me busy at work.

None the less, we still had time to enjoy life at home on days off.

I would often think back to my teenage years … The old gang. We would just get together, smoking cigarettes, drinking beer, listening to music and riding our bikes to the next location where the action would be. Numbering in the twenties we had a main core group of about five or six.

The only club we belonged to was The Claremont Swimming Club. One night a week they held races at the Claremont Baths (except in winter).

In winter I played Rugby Union for the school team. We won every game that year except the Grand Final. Summer was reserved for the beach and body surfing.

> On November 9, 1974, we televised the John Martin's Christmas Pageant in colour. I believe this was the first colour program in South Australia.

On one brief trip back to Perth, my brothers Peter and Nick said that we had been invited to a party. We arrived at the address at the appointed time. The instructions were to enter through the garage and up some stairs. It all seemed very quiet and dark. Then all the lights came on and "SURPRISE".

A group of old friends were there. I looked around at each of them in turn and called them by name: "Mick", "Cuz", "Gandhi", "Maits" ... Then I hit a brick wall. The person standing in front of me was very familiar but I couldn't think where I knew him from or what his name was!

"Who are you?"

"Frank."

FRANK ... Of course, it's Frank. How could I possibly forget Frank! For the last two years of high school we rode our bikes to Claremont together then caught the bus or train to school and back.

I said he had put on weight, that's why I couldn't recognise him.

Yes, he had put on weight – he was always slim – but that wasn't the problem. I had embarrassed both of us in front of everyone.

"You idiot!" I thought.

"Sorry Frank!"

Have you ever had a blank spot in your memory so you can remember a person or place in every detail except the name! No matter how hard you try nothing fits.

Like having the last piece to a Jigsaw puzzle … but it doesn't fit!

During the night "Maits" (Maitland) reminded me how I acquired my nickname. One year in primary school we decided to make up a nickname for everyone in the class, so from Humphry I got "Humphs" then "Humpfrog".

After a swimming race during a school sports day "Maits" said I wasn't old enough to be a frog so I had to be a tadpole. From then on I was called "Taddy" or "Tads". A lot of people didn't know my real name.

That party was the last time I ever saw "Maits". He died a few years later.

It was good to catch up and hear what other people had been doing … but somehow it wasn't the same.

Most of us now have a family and responsibilities … no longer the free and easy life we used to have!

HORSES

Some weekends a small group from SAS would go trail-riding on horseback.

They weren't very good! (The horses that is!)

They were lazy and poorly-trained.

Going away from home, they were reluctant to move and had to be prodded – very firmly! Returning home was the reverse. It was difficult to hold them back to a leisurely pace!

Bill Childs organised the rides. He had some experience with horses. Margie and I joined the group.

After a few sessions we soon learnt quite a lot and we learnt we would be much better with a good horse!

When we began looking to buy a property in the Hills we wanted a place with enough land for a couple of horses. As mentioned earlier, an estate agent, called Pat Coffey, showed us a property called Curragundi, with a hay shed and stables and ten acres of land. Margie remembered often seeing the place when she was a young girl. At that time it was owned by the Master of the Hunt and jumps were set up in the paddocks.

We were able to buy Curragundi at a reasonable price.

Soon after, Bill Childs bought a property at nearby Mount Torrens and then bought a horse to go with it. We looked in the paper each day at horses for sale. One day we found one which would suit us. It was a seven-year-old gelding, quiet, well-trained and trained as a harness horse to pull a buggy around the city.

We went to have a look at him. He was a good size, about fifteen hands, and his name was Danny. We bought Danny and had him delivered. He soon settled in but he would need company.

We were told of a horse for sale at Morphettville, so we went to have a look. He was the same age as Danny, slightly bigger, quiet and well-trained as a trotter.

His name? Danny or Danny boy!

So we decided to call him Dandy. Both horses got on well together from the start.

Buying the horses was the cheap part. Then came saddles, bridles, halters, horse rugs and bills for farriers and vets!

Now we needed a horse float. The best ones were locally made – Taylors' Horse Floats. They were popular, so we were put on a waiting list.

At the same time we were put in contact with Bob Mitton, a distant relative of Margie's. He was a vet and president of the Mountain Pony Club in Mount Barker.

It was a big pony club and they were always on the lookout for adults to supervise young kids, so I was pressured into joining. I always took Dandy with me and we both learned quite a lot.

Every summer the pony club held a camp on Hindmarsh Island.

Due to work commitments I could only go for two days. On my first day Bob suggested that any adults not involved in cooking or other domestic duties could go on an extended ride around the island.

> ” Buying the horses was the cheap part. Then came saddles, bridles, halters, horse rugs and bills for farriers and vets!

It was an interesting ride, but by the end of it Dandy needed a rest. So did I!

The next day I planned to leave late afternoon allowing enough time to drive home, then unpack and clean up. It was a hot day and the Holden station wagon was going to be struggling to tow the horse float up some steep hills.

By the time I packed and loaded my gear, saddle, bridle, halter, hay, a jerrycan of water, and, finally, Dandy, it was getting late. I didn't want to arrive home in the dark, so as soon as I was ready to go I said goodbye to everyone and headed for the ferry into Goolwa.

It was slow-going to Strathalbyn, climbing up from sea level. The radiator temperature was edging higher. From Strath to Mount Barker there are a series of hills and valleys. Going downhill is good, but uphill puts pressure on the engine. I was going to have to stop.

The bottom of the next valley looked good. There was enough room to get off the road and get some shade from a few big trees. Dandy and I would just have to wait for the radiator to cool down before I could put more cold water in it.

> “The boys wanted to learn to ride the horses but they were not big enough ... so we looked for a pony.

There was still a hot, dry wind, so I couldn't leave Dandy shut in the horse float. He appreciated being let out and let me know it. I tied him off to a tree and put some hay within easy reach.

Water was more difficult! I only had a medium-sized bowl so there was a lot of wastage and I had to keep enough for the radiator. We had to wait more than an hour for the radiator to cool down before we could fill it with cold water and load Dandy back on the float.

It was dark when I pulled into our driveway.

Danny heard me lowering the tailgate of the horse float and called out! Dandy responded and both horses were getting excited. Danny ran up and down the fence jumping and kicking up his heels. Both of them calling out to each other!

The situation was getting dangerous.

I got a biscuit of hay from the float and threw it into the paddock, away from the gate to distract Danny. With Danny distracted, I led Dandy through the gate and turned him around facing the gate – a safety measure I had been taught by two very knowledgeable horsemen!

When I unclipped the lead rope he had to turn around before rushing into the paddock to meet Danny.

They galloped off together in the dark!

Our two sons, Ben and Matt, had grown up with horses (as well as donkeys, kangaroos, wombats, possums, sugar gliders, hopping mice, guinea pigs, goats, bats, peacocks and so on … not to mention dogs and a cat!). The boys wanted to learn to ride the horses but they were not big enough … so we looked for a pony.

We bought a small black pony and the boys named him Solo after the Star Wars character. He was all black except for one white patch in the middle of his back. In time, he changed from black to grey to white.

”
We bought a small black pony and the boys named him Solo after the Star Wars character.

Solo hadn't been trained at all. We managed to train him in a few things but he was a stubborn little pony and there were things he just wouldn't do.

We mentioned this to a friend, Clem Wilson.

Clem was one of the best horse trainers in the country. He was also a well-respected, and regular, member of the Harness Horses Section at the Royal Adelaide Show for many years.

Clem Wilson relaxing during a break when filming "Robbery Under Arms"

Matthew on Solo

Among other things, Clem trained horses for several movies including "Ned Kelly" and "Robbery Under Arms".

Clem offered to help with Solo and within minutes he had the pony doing just what we wanted. Ben and Matt learnt to ride on Solo and Matt joined a local pony club.

When we were told TAFE ran a Farrier and Blacksmith course, Margie and I enrolled in it. The classes were held at night during winter.

Sometimes the class was held at a blacksmith forge in Summertown where we would learn to shape iron into horse shoes and other items. Other nights we went to a horse stud at Williamstown to learn how to trim a horse's feet and also how to nail shoes to a horse's feet.

Our horses didn't wear shoes because they were only ever on soft ground.

I did trim them for a while but the novelty wore off – there were other jobs for us to do, so we paid a farrier to do it!

Danny and Dandy had very little exercise for a long time, so when two friends offered to regularly exercise the horses we thought that was a good thing.

Ten acres of land wasn't a big area for a good ride and if they rode on the roads the horses would have to be shod.

They approached the owner of the property opposite, Bill King, and asked if they could ride on his land. Bill had one hundred acres and was the biggest land holder in the Stirling district. He fattened cattle on his land but treated them like family pets.

He agreed to let our friends ride on his property. One time when they came to ride they said that Danny was shaking and agitated, so the ride was cancelled.

We called the vet and after careful examination he said Danny was scared.

He had been pushed too hard!

From then on, Danny and Dandy were left in peace to live out the rest of their lives.

FAMILY TIES

The ties between SAS and TVW were still quite strong when TVW arranged for the Miss Universe program to be held in Perth, in 1979.

They needed our Mercedes OB van to record several segments of the main program and then to borrow our colour cameras for the final at the Perth Entertainment Centre.

Mike McAuliffe and I drove the van to Perth and recorded Miss Universe segments at Kings Park and The Narrows Bridge.

Because TVW's cameras were all tied up we were also asked to record several news interviews with footballer Barry Cable.

A few days before the main program the U.S. Skylab satellite came out of orbit and re-entered the earth's atmosphere. Part of it survived and landed near Rawlinna, east of Kalgoorlie. The remains of the satellite were brought to the Perth Entertainment Centre and included in the Miss Universe program.

While in Perth I had to attend to another matter – our Basset Hound called Huckleberry.

Huckleberry was a good dog. She had had a litter of thirteen pups, but now she was suffering from a severe case of glaucoma. One eye was glazed over and the other eye was starting to do the same. Our vet couldn't do anything to help but said there was a specialist vet in Perth who might be able to do something.

Since I was going to be in Perth it was an opportunity too good to miss. Margie rang the Perth vet and made an appointment, then she put 'Huck' on a plane to Perth.

I drove out to Perth Airport to pick up Huck and arrived just after the plane landed. She was on the tarmac in a wire cage whimpering and looking miserable as only a Bassett Hound can!

I took her back to my parents' place where I was staying in Perth. I kept the appointment with the Perth vet, who took one look at Huck and said she was too far gone and there was nothing he could do about it!

I didn't like the thought of Huck on another plane trip, so I asked Mike if he would object to having Huck in the OB van with us on the trip back to Adelaide. Mike was happy to have Huck and they got on well together.

When the time came to leave, we packed the van with cameras and lenses, and I made up a bed on the floor of the van for Huck.

Miss Universe segment, 1979

Huckleberry with her pups

We met up with Channel 10's Ray Yates and Trevor, a TVW employee with a bus driver's licence. SAS's double-decker bus and OB van with trailer and generator were to travel together.

The bus had a maximum speed of about 30 mph (50 kph). Mike and I would drive ahead during the day then meet the others at a pre-arranged town at night. Whenever we stopped for a break, I would take Huck for a walk and give her a drink.

Most motels won't allow dogs inside.

What they don't know won't hurt them! Huck was very well house-trained.

Just before I went to bed I would smuggle her from the van to the motel room. Our first overnight stop was Norseman. By the time we got to Kalgoorlie we were about two hours ahead of the bus, so Mike and I took a guided tour of an unused gold mine. Being co-driver of the OB van from Adelaide to Perth and back showed Mike's determination.

As a child he suffered from Polio, the result leaving him with one leg shorter than the other. He wore a built-up shoe on his right foot and walked with a limp.

His determined streak, coupled with a great sense of humour, showed up at Cocklebiddy. We had an overnight stop there, and after dinner we were sitting in the lounge bar having a few drinks. We were joined by the two women who ran the motel.

One of the women suggested playing charades and Mike was quick to volunteer to act out a part! He took a broom from behind the bar and began walking backwards, all the while sweeping the floor where he had just been.

Nobody could guess the answer … so Mike said he was an Irish Minesweeper!

His charade was made even better as he dragged his built-up boot behind him!

Mike had a great sense of humour and a lot of courage, as well as being a talented technical operator.

Our last overnight stop was Kimba.

We would have been a couple of hours ahead of the bus, so we waited and waited but they didn't turn up.

In the morning there was still no sign of them. There was no way to contact them, so we decided to go on alone to Adelaide and make enquiries there.

When we arrived at the Station, Mike drove around to the OB garage. I got out of the van and opened the door to the garage, and there was the double-decker bus!

Ray and Trevor had decided to drive all night to beat us home.

The South Australian side of the Eyre Highway was finally sealed!

A joint program was planned by SAS and TVW at the town of Border Village near Eucla.

SAS provided the OB van with a TR60 tape machine and an Ikegami link. TVW supplied three cameras. Bob Pratt and I represented SAS while TVW provided the main part of the crew. We linked to a nearby Telecom tower and patched into the bearer system for both SAS and TVW.

Our first program on SAS was "Earlybirds" with Jane Reilly. After a suitable delay, due to time difference, we repeated the program for TVW with their host. Then we packed up and headed for Wigunda, about 90 kilometres away, for the official opening of the sealed road.

OB van and double-decker bus meet at the border

When we finished recording the official opening, Bob and I drove back to Border Village.

Unfortunately, a strong headwind slowed us down, and we only just made it back in time to replay the program to air!

That night we televised "In Eucla Tonight" live to SAS and TVW. It was a variety program compered by Stuart Wagstaff.

Word had gone out on CB radio, and semi-trailer trucks lined both sides of the road for hundreds of metres!

Dozens of truckies filled the main amenities room of Border Village for a "New Faces" style program. Stuart said he had never felt so intimidated.

The Nullarbor Nymph was resurrected by the crew while we were there!

The Nullarbor Nymph was a hoax initiated by kangaroo hunters near Eucla who claimed they had seen a half-naked woman wrapped in a kangaroo skin running through the bush with kangaroos.

Ever since TVW bought SAS, ties between the two had been strong. TVW sent OB vans to SAS … SAS sent an OB van and staff to Perth for Miss Universe.

This time they met half-way for a joint program … but the old ties were getting weaker!

A LONG DAY

In 1983 the most popular morning radio announcers were Bazz (Barry Ion) and Pilko (Tony Pilkington), and a popular breakfast TV program was "Good Morning Australia" with Gordon Elliott and Kerri-Anne Kennerley.

They decided to have a joint program and called it a simulcast.

I was asked to survey the 5KA radio station to make the necessary technical arrangements.

The audio connections were simple enough but my main concern was the link path from 5KA to Mount Lofty. 5KA was only a two-storey building surrounded by multi-storey buildings. From the roof at one end of the building there was a gap – between the Hilton Hotel and another tall building.

I could set up a microwave link on the roof of 5KA's building, run a coax cable along the roof, down into their maintenance area, to a work bench for the Link Control Unit.

We would need to prepare for an early start the following day!

A 4.30 am start at work meant a three o'clock wake-up at home. Margie and our two boys were still fast asleep, so I tried not to wake them. The weather bureau had predicted it would be an extremely hot, dry, and windy day, and already it was beginning to heat up.

I arrived at 5KA around 4.45 am to set up the Ikegami link, and by six o'clock we were all checked out to Master Control with test signals and communications. The simulcast went smoothly, but I didn't see much of it where I was – there wasn't room in the radio station control room with a camera and lights. At the end of the simulcast we packed up the link, camera, lights and audio equipment and returned to the Studio.

After a meal break we loaded another set of equipment into the truck and drove into the city again to record some segments for a commercial at Yorke Motors.

From Yorke Motors I could see the Adelaide Hills, and didn't like what I saw.

A dust storm was covering the Hills. Someone said a radio station reported that fires had started in the Hills. I was anxious to get home!

We finished the job at Yorke Motors, quickly packed up the equipment and returned to the Station. There was nothing else booked for the day, and it had been an early start, so I headed for home. On the freeway there was little traffic and no signs

Wellington Wombat knew something was wrong

of smoke nearby. One of the first things to do was to check the animals' water containers.

We had about a dozen kangaroos in a one-acre paddock, which was surrounded by a six-foot-high fence. Their main supply of water was a large metal bucket under trees near the highest point on the ten acre property.

A water trough for the horses was close by, with a feed tapped off for Wellington Wombat.

It was all conveniently set up close to a hay shed and stables. But it was a steep walk from the house up to the stables.

While I was filling the Kangaroos' water trough, I could smell smoke! It was a strong smell of burning Eucalypts.

It was coming from Bridgewater, and it was heading our way!

As soon as I had filled the water bucket I hurried downhill, turning on sprinklers as I went.

Water comes from a well and bore next to the creek bed, and is pumped up a two and a half inch pipe to a tank at the highest point on the property. Hoses and sprinklers were permanently set out in the paddocks to keep a green strip around the house. When I reached the house I turned on the pump. The pump could stay on even if the tank overflowed.

It was more important to keep the tank full.

There were several loud explosions coming from Bridgewater.

It had to be fuel tanks at the service station at the top of Germantown Hill!

The fire first appeared on the other side of Mount Barker Road in a property owned by Bill King. His property was probably the largest single land holding in the Stirling Council district.

A cop walking down the road called out and said I had to leave!

I told him I had to open gates to let the animals out.

I opened the gates for the horses and kangaroos. Wellington would be down one of his burrows and would stay there. The horses were in the far paddock and didn't seem to be aware of the danger. The fire rolled down the hill parallel to our property. The sound it made was a low rumble.

> ” It soon became obvious that the fire was moving too fast and getting around us.

Then it jumped the road and headed straight for me!

The horses saw the fire and galloped towards me. Suddenly they turned and jumped over the fire into an area of the paddock that was only low grass. I took the sprinkler off a hose and walked down into the paddock with the hose to the dry creek bed – hoping to stop the fire there.

When I looked back I saw our neighbour Max Pollock coming to help.

A sudden gust of wind made the fire flare up, so I had to drop the hose and run towards the house! Max called out that he had to go to save his own house.

He sounded apologetic because he had to go.

That was Max.

I called out, "Thanks for your help."

It soon became obvious that the fire was moving too fast and getting around us.

I decided to check the house. We had been adding an extension at the side. The concrete floor was already in place and some building rubbish was piled up against the existing wall.

The rubbish had caught fire and would soon spread to the house itself!

So I hosed the rubbish down, and then moved it onto the middle of the concrete floor.

I walked around the house several times looking for any fires, but the lawns and gardens had done their job.

Unfortunately, the hay shed and stables were gone.

They were just a pile of twisted iron. There were two more sheds between the house and the stables. One was an old milking shed made of bricks and asbestos. It was safe. The second shed was very open and contained a lot of old building materials and our horse float at one end.

I wanted to get the horse float out of the shed onto an area of lawn. I turned the station wagon around and backed it up to the float. I just had to lift the front of the float up and onto the wagon's tow bar. It was something I had done many times before, but this time when I tried to lift, my legs cramped!

Just then, Max walked up the driveway. He came over to see if I was all right. I said that I was OK and asked how he got on. Max said that he saved the house but he lost his shed with his tractor inside.

Max's tractor meant a great deal to him. He had spent a lot of time and effort on it.

Remains of hay shed and stables

Home and paddock protected by massive pine trees

I asked him if he would help me lift the horse float onto the station wagon's towbar. With his help we lifted the float onto the towbar and I drove both the vehicle and horse float onto the lawn.

I wondered if Max could have saved his shed and tractor if he hadn't come to help me!

The main fire had passed and Max went home to put out any spot fires and check fences.

I was about to do the same thing when I heard Margie calling out my name. She came running up the driveway looking distressed and then relieved to see that I was OK.

We held on to each other for a few minutes while Margie told me that the police had stopped her down by the freeway.

One of the cops told her that he told one old man to leave his house, but he had refused! He then said he told another man to leave, but he had said that he had to let the animals out!

One kangaroo had been seen hopping down the road!

We decided to slowly check out the property, so we walked up to where the stables used to be. Wellington came out of one of his burrows. Not a happy wombat!

One kangaroo was missing but the rest were still in their paddock, so I shut the gate and propped up a burnt fence post.

The sprinklers had stopped so I assumed the power must be off. We were lucky to still have mains water and two tanks of rainwater.

I showed Margie where a fire had started in a pile of building rubbish.

It was only because we had a simulcast with Bazz and Pilko that morning that I had begun work early and finished early.

Three hungry horses in a burnt paddock

That meant I was home to put out the fire. Otherwise the house would have burnt down!

It was the only spot fire I had seen close to the house. In the paddock I had seen a lot of burning leaves flying through the air.

On closer inspection we found that the fire had stopped at a line of pine trees and was still smouldering under the trees.

The pine trees had been planted in an "L" shape covering the north and west sides of the house.

They were more than 100 years old. Luckily I had trimmed the lower branches and slashed the grass under the trees.

We had been told that pines had to heat up to an ignition temperature before they would burn. As long as there was no undergrowth to feed the fire into the trees they were safe. The pines then stopped any spot fires.

Our two boys had been kept safe at school in Hahndorf. A few friends came to see if they could help.

The horses looked pathetic standing in a burnt-out paddock so we ordered a truckload of hay.

"Looks like takeaway for dinner tonight."

It had been A VERY LONG DAY!

That was Ash Wednesday (February 16, 1983).

The next morning, a kangaroo was hopping up and down the fence trying to get in!

WORKING WITH DON

It was 1972, the year of the large-scale outdoor rock concerts and festivals.

Adelaide's was held on a farm near the town of Meadows.

The Meadows Technicolor Fair.

When we first did a survey of the location it was just a paddock with a few clumps of trees and a dam.

The main stage was to be next to a group of trees facing an open paddock.

By walking away a few hundred metres from the stage and sighting up our Transmitter tower at Mount Lofty, I could see a scaffold tower ten metres high would be required for a line-of-sight link path.

We had a scaffold tower built about twenty metres from the front of the stage. On the first day of the concert I parked the International Harvester OB van next to the scaffold tower and set up a microwave link on the top of the tower.

The van had a platform on the roof with a mounting for a camera. We could continuously send live pictures of the concert back to the Studio.

On the second day of the concert the zoom lens on the camera stopped working!

I didn't have any circuits or test equipment in the van so I called the Studio to say I would be coming back.

A few minutes later the chief engineer, Don Caddy, called me and said the Transmitter building at Mount Lofty was much closer and he would meet me there.

When I arrived at the Transmitter the front door was open and a workbench cleared ready to work. We set up the camera and zoom lens on the workbench and, with the aid of a circuit diagram and various test points, it didn't take long to trace the fault and fix it!

I said, "Thanks" to Don and returned to the Meadows Technicolor Fair.

The Transmitter building at Mount Lofty is often useful for Outside Broadcasts.

For the Australian Men's Hardcourt Tennis at Memorial Drive we had three link paths from Memorial Drive via Mount Lofty to SAS Studio and then on to Melbourne. There were two Outgoing Links (a Main and a Backup) and one Return Link.

We set up and checked all links a few days before the tournament.

In the morning on the first day of the tournament, the Melbourne director arrived at the OB. Graeme was considered to be their best sporting director.

After checking the camera positions he said, "The two courtside cameras have to be moved to the other side of the court."

"Why?"

"Because in Melbourne and Sydney the courtside cameras are on the right side of the court as seen by Camera 2, and we want to keep the same look going from one state to another."

By tradition, Camera 2 is always the main wide-shot camera. In a three camera studio arrangement, Cameras 1 and 3 cross-shoot close-ups, while Camera 2 is the wide-shot (safe) camera. So the crew moved the courtside cameras to the right-hand side (east side) of the court.

When the commentators arrived they were seated in a host position to rehearse the opening segment of the telecast. They would use information and statistics from the return link by watching a monitor.

"Where's the return link?" asked Graeme. I switched the return link on to a monitor … there was no picture, no noise, just a flat line on the waveform monitor!

I called SAS Master Control and asked them to check if there was a picture going out on the return link. "We need that return link," called Graeme.

"On it," I called back. Then Master Control said there was definitely a picture going out on the return link from SAS to Mount Lofty, and Don Caddy was on his way up to the Mount (Lofty).

We had hired ADS Channel 10's van for the tennis because our Mercedes van was too small. In the ADS van the technical and production areas are in separate compartments.

Meadow's Technicolor Fair

Graeme stepped into the Technical section and said, "Do you realise that in less than half an hour we go live to the whole of the east coast of Australia?"

I replied, "Thanks!" Then to myself, "You're a big help!"

Graeme said, "Can't you borrow a link from Channel 9?"

So I said, "Even if we could, it would take hours to set it up." Graeme went back to the production section of the van to rehearse the opening segment without the return link!

> "
> I worked with Don on several problems. Always with good results!

Don phoned me from the Mount Lofty Transmitter building and told me he was receiving a return link picture from SAS. He suggested we could switch to the secondary frequency.

I had spent a lot of time with these Ikegami links, so I said I didn't think that would help! This was because we were receiving a strong signal level but no modulation, just a flat line. A typical patching problem.

I then asked Don if he would check the video monitor output on the Link Control Unit.

After a few seconds, Don said he checked it and there was a video signal.

Only one more place to check, and that was a video monitor output on the Link Head. The link head was mounted behind the Link Dish, which was on a purpose-built platform on the roof of the building.

I asked Don if he would look at this monitoring point. Don said OK, and it took only a couple of minutes to run a video cable from the roof to the control room. Once again there was a video signal. There was only one point further on, which could possibly remove the video signal. It was the Modulation Level Control.

But that would mean dismantling the head unit and there wasn't time.

Don said, "I really think we should change frequency …" I said, "Yes, OK," although I couldn't see how that could make any difference. I pushed the switch to change to the secondary frequency.

> He will always be remembered as a gentleman and a friend. ”

On the return link monitor there was a burst of noise then a picture appeared.

"Thank you, Don! You were right from the start!"

Don said, "Don't hesitate to call me if you have any other problems."

"Thanks again, Don."

I called Graeme on the talkback, "You've got return link back."

No response!

The team began their rehearsal again.

The tennis was to be played under lights, commencing just before sundown. As the players came out on court Graeme called for pictures from all cameras.

The two courtside cameras on the east side of the court looking west were shooting straight into the sun.

They couldn't be used for the first half hour of the match.

At the end of the tournament we packed up all the equipment and left the cables for the next day. Then the crew relaxed by having a few drinks courtside, until security moved us on!

When all cables had been picked up and equipment stored away, I set up the offending link on the maintenance bench.

With power on, I switched the link to its primary frequency. The link worked perfectly, so I left it running on the bench and went on with other work.

A few hours later I checked the link and the fault was back!

A video signal was connected to the link transmitter but nothing was coming out of the receiver. On the bench it was much easier to track down the source! The receiver was generating its own signal, replacing the wanted one.

Fixing the problem could take a little longer!

I was working on it when Don came into the maintenance area. When I explained what had caused the fault he just laughed and moved on!

I worked with Don on several problems. Always with good results!

He will always be remembered as a gentleman and a friend.

BIRDMAN

The first Birdman Rally was held on the River Torrens at Pinky Flat. A lot of damage was done to council gardens and school boat sheds by spectators. It wasn't a very suitable location, so the next year the producer decided to hold it at the Patawalonga.

A scaffold platform was to be attached to the bridge across the Patawalonga River. Some bright spark decided the best way to do this was to build the scaffold platform on pontoons on one bank of the 'Pat' then float the platform down to the bridge.

When the scaffold platform was finished it was so heavy the riggers could not move it off the bank and into the water! They asked me if I could help. I had a long, heavy-duty rope we used for hauling equipment up towers.

We attached one end of the rope to the scaffold platform then ran the rope across the "Pat" to the opposite bank. We

The new Toyota Hiace van

then attached the other end to the towbar of the International Harvester van. With the van in four wheel drive and low gear ratio I slowly moved forward.

The rope stretched a bit before the scaffold started to move. Once it started to move it was hard to stop, and it gained momentum as it entered the water. As soon as the scaffold was floating on the pontoons in the water the whole thing fell over on its side!

The whole structure was top heavy and unstable. Everyone involved went ducking for cover and blaming everyone else!

Two months later the Birdman Rally was held at Glenelg for the first time. It became a very successful event and represented a lot of effort packed into just one day. Whereas golf can run for several days.

On one South Australian Golf Open we had up to three people smoking cigarettes in the confined space of the Mercedes OB van at the same time!

The next day our audio operator, Steve Stevens, turned up wearing a gas mask! He also took advantage of being able to organise a breathing tube to hang out the back door of the van. It was part joking and part serious!

I talked to Assistant Chief Engineer John Stankovich about the problem. “Stanky” brought up the subject at the next Executive Meeting, but he was over-ruled by the smoking executives.

It was a few years before smoking was banned in the OB van.

A new facility was added to the OB garage. It was a Toyota Hiace van with a BCN20 videotape machine and TK76 camera.

It was basically a very portable version of the old International Harvester van.

The Hiace van was mostly used for commercials by VizAd.

In the next six years we averaged 150 jobs per year. Then two additions changed the use of the Hiace van: the Betacam camera and the Gold Rod link.

With a portable 2 GHz link and Gold Rod antenna, the Hiace van was used for live news crosses. The Hiace van was made available for news from 3 pm onwards. One of the very first 'mobile' phones was installed in the van. The mobile phone was a briefcase-size unit, mounted on the side of the van and connected to the vehicle's battery. It was modified to give an audio feed for earbuds.

Despite the extra room offered by the Hiace van with a Betacam camera, production crews still preferred to use a station wagon.

When Christopher Skase bought out TVW he also acquired SAS. So he owned Channel 7 in every state except South Australia where SAS was Channel 10!

With SAS aligned with the Seven Network, ADS 7 was aligned with the Ten Network.

It was decided SAS and ADS would switch channels, so SAS 10 became SAS 7 and ADS 7 became ADS 10.

The changed occurred on December 27, 1987.

As SAS and ADS transmitters were located in a shared building, initial changeover was relatively easy.

Video and audio cables were run between transmitters which meant SAS was transmitting on ADS's transmitter and ADS on SAS's transmitter. Later, the two transmitters were re-tuned, so SAS and ADS used their own transmitters.

We televised the Christmas Pageant for almost 30 years – always on the first Saturday in November.

In 1985 Adelaide hosted its first Grand Prix on the same weekend, and the Nine Network circus rolled into town.

On the Friday we ran cables, rigged and checked two links on John Martins' car-park roof. The links were set to their primary frequencies (7160 MHz and 7370 MHz). After a 6 am start on the Saturday we switched on the van and turned on the links.

A short time later, Master Control called on the radio to tell me that there was interference on one of the links.

I changed to the secondary frequency on that link and Master Control said it was clean. A few minutes later Master Control called to say Channel 9 was on the phone claiming that one of our links was causing interference to one of their links and demanded we shut down our links!

I told Master Control to tell Channel 9 we would change back to our primary frequency as soon as they switched off any links (which were on secondary frequencies) adjacent to our primaries.

We never heard back from them!

Typical 'bully boy' tactics from Nine's interstate crews.

Under the Link Frequency Licence Regulations, if a link on a secondary frequency causes interference to a link on a primary frequency, then the link on the secondary frequency must shut down!

THE RIGHT PLACE AT THE RIGHT TIME

SAS bought a battery-powered 2 GHz link with a two foot cylindrical antenna. The antenna was painted bright yellow, and the whole thing was referred to as the Gold Rod. A wooden box was made to house the Gold Rod, battery pack, monitor, audio equipment and cables.

VIZ-AD made the most use of the production van but the Newsroom wanted to use the Gold Rod with the Hiace van for live news crosses so the van was used for program and commercial production up to 3 pm. After 3 pm the van was made available for news. The Gold Rod box was very heavy and required two people to lift it in or out of the Hiace van, so it was often left in the van.

We had just finished recording segments for a commercial in Glenelg and I was driving the Hiace van up Anzac Highway to return to the Studio when the phone rang. It was the Newsroom.

Chris said, "Have you got the Gold Rod with you?"

"Yes."

"Where are you?"

"On Anzac Highway at the intersection of Cross Road."

"We need you to go to the State Government Office building on Victoria Square to set up the Gold Rod on the 11th floor as quickly as possible."

"OK, but parking can be difficult in that area."

"There's a parking area at the rear of the building. Access to it is by a laneway off Gawler Place. We have a contact there. I'll ask him to keep an eye out for you."

It would have to be a big news story to want a link out early in the afternoon.

I drove up Anzac Highway, West Terrace, Grote Street, through Victoria Square to Gawler Place and found the laneway! A man was waiting for me and indicated to park next to the rear entrance of the State Government Office building.

He showed me how to get to the lifts and then gave me directions to get to a media room on the 11th floor. For the first load I carried the Gold Rod, tripod and battery pack. It wasn't a very big room, with a lectern in the centre of one end.

The only window was a narrow window in one corner of the room. It was double glass with louvres in between the glass panels. The louvres could be adjusted with a suitable Allen key and they had been set with the slats approximately horizontal.

Through the window I could see the Transmitter tower at Mount Lofty.

I went back to the van to get another load. This time it was a large plastic container filled with a Test-Signal Generator, Audio Mixer, microphones and cables. When I got back to the room a cameraman and journalist had arrived.

I set up the link tripod in front of the window and attached the Gold Rod and link to it. I then connected the battery, test generator and audio mixer to the link and switched it on. With the link turned on, I phoned Master Control and asked them to look for the link signal. Master Control has a remote control to pan and tilt the receiver on the tower at Mount Lofty.

After a few minutes Master Control called back and said that they could only find a very weak signal. I told them about the window and the louvres, and then said that I would try a few adjustments and call back.

Microwaves can behave in a strange way if there are obstacles in the path. Depending on the dimensions of the obstacle and the signal path, the combined signal can be in phase and increase the signal, or out of phase and cancel.

After raising the tripod about an inch, I called Master Control and asked if the signal had improved. They said it had improved a lot and please don't change anything!

I ran the video cable to the Channel 7 camera, plugged it in, and then attached a microphone to the lectern. The room had been steadily filling and was quite crowded. I made one more hurried trip to the van to get the portable TV receiver/monitor.

When I returned, I saw a man in a dustcoat holding a toolbox and looking at the window. I hurried over and asked

Adjusting the Gold Rod

what he wanted. He said he'd been asked to adjust the louvres by Channel 7.

I said it had all been fixed and please don't change anything!

He was a bit doubtful about that and said he had been told to speak to Mike from Channel 7. So I showed him my card which seemed to satisfy him! I then settled down to protect my corner of the room and the equipment. Our cameraman was in contact with the studio by phone, keeping them informed. A journalist near the door announced "he" was coming!

"They switched to live pictures of Bannon stepping up to the lectern to announce that he was resigning as Premier ...

I recognised the voice of the Premier, John Bannon, as he entered the room and stopped to speak to some of the journalists he knew.

On my TV receiver I could see Graeme Goodings in the Studio explaining we were cutting into normal programming for a special Government announcement.

They switched to live pictures of Bannon stepping up to the lectern to announce that he was resigning as Premier because of the State Bank collapse!

It was a brief but sad moment.

As Bannon left the room, cameramen and journalists rushed to be the first to spread the news.

We had already beaten them!

Channel 9 and 10 had their link vans parked next to my van in the rear car park. They would replay the recorded announcement delayed by only a few minutes. Who would notice or care? I had often argued with the Newsroom that a portable link was more versatile and more useful than a fixed link van.

I had spoken to John Bannon briefly on two occasions before.

The first was in the backyard of his house in Prospect – waiting for the election results.

The second was at the Christmas Pageant.

Patsy Biscoe arrived at our commentary position wearing a brief leather miniskirt. I said she was supposed to have been told to wear jeans to climb the scaffold steps to the commentary platform.

She just said, "I don't wear jeans!" As she began to climb the steps I thought I should look away. John Bannon standing next to me said, "Ah, a gentleman!"

And he did the same thing.

He *was* a gentleman!

CRUISER

When SAS bought a 2 GHz transmitter and Gold Rod it put the Channel ahead of the other stations for live news crosses!

To catch up, Channel 9 and Channel 10 bought link vans.

A link van typically has an antenna mounted on a pan-and-tilt head on top of a telescopic mast, which can be extended by compressed air, and a 2 GHz transmitter.

Our Newsroom felt we were being left behind and aggressively pushed for a similar van.

In practice, I can't think of a single occasion when their link vans could get a link path out and our Hiace van couldn't.

On the other hand, there were times when a portable link was a definite advantage.

The Newsroom heard of a News Cruiser (ATN link van) in ATN's car park, which was not being used. Without telling anyone at SAS the Newsroom asked ATN to send the Cruiser to Adelaide. ATN was glad to get rid of it. It was an embarrassment!

Eventually we got our own News Cruiser. The bodywork, mast, rack frame and vehicle electrics were done in Sydney by the same company which did ATN's Cruisers.

Trevor Lanyon and I drove the Cruiser back to Adelaide where I installed the electronics. The Cruiser was newer and better than the other link vans in Adelaide. By the late 1990s we were averaging more than 300 news crosses per year.

In September '92 Chief Engineer Don Caddy asked me if I would like to go to Japan for Camera Acceptance Tests at Hitachi.

One person from each state (two from Sydney) was invited to attend. We travelled from our hotel to the Hitachi factory by train, together with millions of Japanese workers! At each station we could see hundreds of bicycles lined up outside … the normal means of travel in Japan … and no graffiti to be seen! Although the tests were for F3 and F300 cameras, technicians from Sydney and Melbourne were more interested in the F700.

They complained that the line-up procedure in the manual didn't work!

Hitachi engineers arranged a special session with one of their technicians to demonstrate the line-up procedure. We were each given a photocopy of line-up procedure in the manual.

The line-up demonstrated by their tech was very different to their manual. The sequence of steps was different and several new steps were included! I re-numbered the steps and included the new ones as best I could.

SA Telecasters Don Caddy

Back at SAS I went through the steps together with the circuit diagrams and it began to make sense.

So I wrote a new line-up procedure!

Our Camera Maintenance Technician Jenny Waldram tried the new line-up procedure and it worked, so she sent a copy to Sydney and now Sydney and Melbourne use it!

It's good to get some value out of a trip like that.

In 1995 Bill Rowse arranged the purchase of a second-hand satellite trailer and dish.

He then installed the necessary equipment to transmit and receive signals via satellite.

Initially the trailer was towed by a Mitsubishi truck. This was replaced by a Jeep, then by a Toyota Landcruiser.

The SNG (Satellite News Gathering) was used in Tasmania, Bourke, Nullarbor and Woomera and even around Adelaide City where link paths are difficult.

The satellite is located over the equator, so the dish must be pointed a few degrees east of north at an elevation of about 45 degrees.

Because of the physical layout of the dish on the trailer, the back of the trailer must be pointing approximately north. The trailer is more than three and a half metres long and very heavy. It is not always possible to position the SNG at a location and satisfy all of these conditions.

In the city it is generally not possible to use the SNG on roads running east-west. It is usually only possible on the west side of roads running north-south or on one of the five main city squares.

I drove the SNG unit to Nullarbor for a news feed of a pack of sharks eating a dead whale. Returning from Nullarbor I was just south of Port Pirie travelling at about 100 kph (the SNG speed limit recommended by Health & Safety). A car and caravan travelling slightly slower was in front of me, no traffic in the opposite direction, and one car a long way behind me. I moved across to the right hand side of the road and started to pass the car and van. When I was sure I was well clear, I started to move back to the left. A car raced through on the inside with inches to spare. It had to be doing 150 kph or more!

I quickly straightened up to avoid a collision. The SNG trailer began to fishtail and for a few seconds I thought it was going to flip over!

Fortunately it stabilised. It took a few minutes for me to calm down.

Sometime later, just south of Virginia, the speeding car was abandoned in a paddock. I assumed it was a stolen car taken for a joy ride!

LOST IT

Our most regular live news cross was from Football Park. Almost every week during the football season we were down there at the same location.

The Channel 7 position was well established.

It was in line with the centre of the ground, raised up so the fans who came to watch their team practice couldn't stand behind the journalist or guest and pull faces during filming of those segments.

We weren't blocking an access or stairs or running cables where people could trip on them (a major complaint by Stadium Management). It was also close to a convenient link path and power outlets.

The setup was fairly straightforward but it meant several trips from the car park. The link was the battery-powered Gold Rod on a tripod. Video and audio cables were run a short distance from the link to a colour bar generator and an audio mixer. Two microphones were connected to the mixer with headphones for monitoring. A modified mobile phone provided Interrupted Fold Back (IFB) with a splitter and volume control feeding the IFB to the guest and cameraman. Finally a TV receiver/monitor was placed on a stand a few metres in front of the guest.

> “My instincts told me he was trouble.

I always allowed plenty of time to check out the system. The link had to be checked through to Master Control. IFB was checked by calling Telstra's recorded time. Microphones and TV receiver were tested. Normally I would be finished testing the system before the cameraman arrived. All that was left was to set up the camera and lights. The power outlet was about five metres away.

On one particular occasion, I had one more trip to the van to get the TV receiver and its stand when the cameraman arrived.

He was a new cameraman on his first "Live Cross" at Football Park, so I stopped to point out where the guest would be and where the power outlet was. Then I went to the van to get the TV receiver and monitor stand. When I returned I saw that the camera and lights had been set up about three metres to one side of our position. For a few seconds I didn't know what to think.

Was this a practical joke?

The new cameraman said that it was closer to the power!

Did he really expect me to pack up everything, move to a new position and set it up again, and then check it all out again?

All that to save running just an extra three or four metres of power cable!

I said, "It's no good having the camera over there when the guest is over here, the microphones are over here, the earbuds are over here, and the feed to the link is over here."

He had also set up on a set of stairs blocking an emergency exit!

He soon got the message and moved the camera and lights.

My instincts told me he was trouble.

His name was Robin Brown and I had several problems working with him. He would make unreasonable demands just to suit himself.

Another regular live news cross was from the steps of Parliament House. It was a difficult location to get a link path back to the Station. For a while we used the Satellite News Gathering (SNG) unit from the plaza area at the back of Parliament House. It meant driving the SNG unit across the footpath and running video and audio cables along the edge of the footpath, up the side of Parliament House.

In June 1997, I tore the ligaments in my right shoulder and had to have a shoulder reconstruction.

After about six weeks I was allowed to return to work with light duties, which meant I wasn't allowed to lift anything heavy.

As fate would have it, the Newsroom wanted a new Live Cross from Parliament House. I was the only person available who knew how to operate the SNG.

At that time it required two fit men to lift the generator on and off the SNG trailer (Bill Rowse later installed a winch on the trailer to lift the generator making it a one-man job). I was not allowed to help lift the generator. Two other men would be required. Cameraman Greg Dunstan was one and Chris Gray was rostered on for the night as the second person to lift the generator.

> "
> I was cold and wet and ANGRY.

It was a bitterly cold, wet August night when I drove the SNG into the city and onto the plaza. Greg and Chris lifted the generator off the trailer. I could manage the rest of the SNG setup with my left arm. Greg set up his camera and lights and Chris ran the video and audio cables from the SNG to the front of Parliament House.

The light rain continued and I already had a cold. Despite a thick heavy jumper, it was still freezing! We finished the Live Cross without any problems and got the "all clear" from the Station to shut down.

I shut down the SNG unit and started to pack up when a Channel 7 News car drove across the footpath onto the edge of the plaza. Robin Brown leaned out of the car door and said there was some police action on the other side of town and he needed someone to operate the link van.

Could he take Chris?

I said, "No, he has to lift the generator onto the trailer!"

Brown backed the car out, and I went back to locking down the satellite dish. When I had finished packing up the SNG I went looking for Greg and Chris. I found Greg on the steps of Parliament House and asked where Chris was. Greg told me Chris got into Robin Brown's car and left.

I was stunned. Chris' sole purpose was to lift the generator onto the trailer!

I wasn't allowed to lift anything and Greg couldn't lift the generator on his own. There wasn't any point in Greg staying, so I asked him to go back to the Station and get two people to come back and lift the generator. I was getting angry with both Brown and Chris Gray.

From his past record I could understand Brown was capable of doing something like this but Chris Gray knew it was essential he stay to lift the generator! As I walked back to the SNG I noticed that the video and audio cables were still run out along the edge of the footpath, so I started to wind up the cables onto their reels.

> " I had lost control. I had lost the moral high ground. I had lost the advantage. I had lost respect.

It wasn't easy with one hand, especially with my left hand!

The rain began again. Not heavy, but a steady light rain which soon began to soak through my jumper.

Once the cables were wound up, I loaded them onto the trailer then sat in the vehicle. I was cold and wet and ANGRY.

I started the engine and turned up the heater and waited and stewed over what had happened. Greg had plenty of time to go back to the Station and get some help. I was tempted to drive off and leave the generator.

It seemed to take a very long time and I was beginning to wonder if I was going to have to spend the night there. All the time getting more and more angry.

Without any warning a news car pulled up, and getting out of the car were Robin Brown and Keith Smith. At the sight of Brown I lost it and told him just what I thought of him.

The stream of abuse lasted for thirty seconds or more. Then Keith said, "Cut it out Mike." I have a lot of respect for Keith, so that helped me to snap out of it.

Then I realised that I had lost it.

I had lost control.

I had lost the moral high ground. I had lost the advantage. I had lost respect. That was a bad mistake. It was OK to be angry and to let Robin know that I was angry but I should have kept control. There would probably be repercussions.

The next morning I was asked to go to the Operations office. When I got there I found Dave Bates and Trevor Lanyon waiting.

I had expected some criticism about the previous night, but they were more concerned about my shoulder. Had I kept to light duties?

It seems that I was not the only one who had trouble with Robin Brown!

BURNT OUT

Football Park was pre-cabled for AFL football.

The cable ends were coiled up in a padlocked box attached to the outside wall of the stadium.

I would back up the OB van to the stadium next to the cable box. We would then connect the cables to the van and turn on power.

One day when I switched on power I could smell smoke, but it soon dissipated. It was impossible to tell where the smoke was coming from because of the air-conditioning. The cameras and links hadn't been turned on and the video and audio switchers were working. I guessed that the smoke had come from one of the monitors.

After a while a cameraman came to the van to say he had connected his camera but could neither hear nor talk to anyone.

I checked a couple of talkback panels but there was no background hiss.

When I checked the main talkback unit the power supply was burnt up. The circuit board and components were a charred mess. It could not be repaired. Fortunately it was a single 12 volt supply, feeding all the talkback panels.

> “The burnt out talkback unit was no great loss. We had already ordered a new system and we were just waiting for a suitable time to install it.

Keith Smith was maintenance technician for the day, so I asked him to go back to the Studio and pick up a Lab Power Supply and leads. A short time later a TD (Technical Director) said that a CCU (Camera Control Unit) was indicating “Cam Cable Short”. After unplugging the camera cable the CCU still indicated a short. I left a message for Smithy to pick up the spare maintenance CCU as well as the lab power supply. There were a few other problems to fix.

It was one of those days!

When Smithy returned we connected the lab power supply and turned it on. It immediately shut down indicating “Overcurrent Protection”. A meter showed a short circuit across the terminals.

Should have thought of that, shouldn’t I?

The power supply should have been fused or protected. The DC power is distributed to the talkback panels by a number of multicore cables connected to the back of the main unit. I disconnected cables until the short disappeared. It was the cable to the directors panel. There were some spare cables in the system so we were able to bypass the faulty cable. We got it fixed during rehearsal … 20 minutes before we were due to go on air!

The burnt out talkback unit was no great loss. We had already ordered a new system and we were just waiting for a suitable time to install it. The old system came with Sydney's OB 2 van, to be upgraded for AFL.

When Football Park opened in 1974 it was the centrepiece of South Australian football.

The grandstand would only be full for SANFL finals. Then the Crows entered the AFL in 1991, followed by Port Adelaide in 1997. Media interest and requirements increased dramatically.

The media made claim to areas at the back of the grandstand next to the timekeepers. They marked out their territory with platforms, desks and chairs. This was divided up by the huge concrete supports for the roof.

These concrete supports were spaced every few metres along the back of the grandstand and extended from the back wall of the grandstand into the last few rows of seating. They formed a natural partition for the media. Access to the area was up the centre grandstand stairs, then branching out to the front of the media boxes in a path that would challenge a mountain goat!

Football Park Management decided it was time to upgrade the media facilities. They called a meeting with representatives from the media. Football Director Greg Packer was nominated to represent Channel 7. The day before the meeting Greg asked me if I had any suggestions or requests to put to the meeting, and if so could I let him know the following day.

Access to the media area was always the biggest problem. The concrete supports for the roof had always prevented access from the rear of the media boxes, rather than the front. The problem would be solved if it was possible to build a walkway behind the back wall of the grandstand and concrete roof supports. Whether that was possible or practical would be up to the architects but it was worth a suggestion.

> “The Hiace van had been very useful for hundreds of commercials and hundreds of live news crosses. Now it was due for replacement.

A lift had been suggested before, especially by the crew who carry heavy equipment up and down the stairs (they counted the number of steps). In this case a lift would be included with the walkway. I drew a diagram showing the concrete supports, the rear wall of the grandstand, a walkway and a lift. One entrance from the stairs to the walkway would be needed in case of fire.

Wheelchair access to the media area would be possible, and a toilet would be greatly appreciated by commentators who can't leave their position for long! A walkway at the rear would take up less paying customer seats than a front entrance. I also drew a line showing the centre line of the oval to be in line with camera two (the wide shot camera).

I gave the drawings to Greg and explained them to him and the reasons why. There was never any decision made at the meeting, but months later building started on the media upgrades.

They included a walkway behind the rear wall of the grandstand and a lift.

The Hiace van had been very useful for hundreds of commercials and hundreds of live news crosses. Now it was due for replacement.

It had been so successful I assumed it would be replaced by a later model. The head cameraman sent a memo to the station manager saying that a Toyota Tarago would be better than a Toyota Hiace. To back up his request he claimed that:

1. The Tarago had a higher clearance, so it would be more suitable for country roads.
2. The Tarago had a smaller turning circle, so it would be more suitable for parking and tight situations in the city.
3. The Tarago has more storage space for camera, lights and other equipment.

A Toyota dealer was happy to send me the specifications sheets for both vehicles. The Hiace van had higher clearance and smaller turning circle than the Tarago. It was designed as a delivery vehicle. As for storage space, you only had to look at the two vehicles and you could see which one had the most storage space!

The Hiace van was shaped like a box with a low floor level – and there lay the real reason for choosing a Tarago! The Tarago's seats were more comfortable, and it had a stylish body, so the driver looked "cool", not like a delivery driver.

The vehicle was basically a production vehicle, so they were given their choice!

WITTENOOM

One of my favourite memories was my time in Wittenoom.

A company called Australian Blue Asbestos (ABA) operated an asbestos mine and mill at Wittenoom. Each year they offered temporary jobs to university students during their summer holidays. My brother Nick and I applied for, and won, jobs there. At that time the true danger of asbestos was not known!

It was common knowledge that mining could be bad for your health - causing dust in the lungs unless you wore a dust mask. We were warned that a dust mask must be worn at all times on the job. But It wasn't until years later that it was known that asbestos could cause Mesothelioma.

Sixty years later and we are both OK!

Nick didn't stay there very long. He had to return to Perth to sit for supplementary exams.

Company housing area

Waterhole

On site, close to the mill, Management and permanent married employees lived in company houses. Single permanent employees and university students were housed in a motel-style building.

All my meals were supplied, but the rooms were small and not air-conditioned. I couldn't cool down with a shower because the water was fed through a metal pipe above ground from a nearby spring. The water didn't cool down until after dark.

The only way to cool down was to head to a waterhole about three hundred metres away. After dinner we would walk to the "Wittenoom Club". It was just an iron shed full of beer!

Staggering back to the rooms it was useful to have a torch! Once the sun went down the sky was lit up with stars and it was easy to pick out The Southern Cross and Two Pointers to find south.

In my room I was often visited by lizards or huntsman spiders. One day I provoked a huntsman with my thong. It responded by sinking its fangs into my thong, leaving a permanent puncture mark! I'm told they are harmless … if you leave them alone!

During my days off I would go for long walks up and out of the gorge. Sometimes I would meet kangaroos or lizards. From one point I could see the mine entrance and mill.

The entrance to the mine was high up, near the top of the gorge. The ore comes out of the mine on a conveyor belt to a picking shed, where rocks which have no sign of asbestos are removed. The ore with asbestos is then crushed, and rocks and rubble are removed. After a few more stages of treatment all that is left is asbestos. The asbestos coming out of the mill looked like giant blue cottonwool balls.

Asbestos mine and mill

Joffre Falls

The company housing was located only a few kilometres from the mine. The workers all lived at the town of Wittenoom, which was at the end of the gorge and more than ten kilometres from the mine.

The beginning of the gorge is called Joffre Falls and is not accessible from the lower part. To get there meant driving out of the gorge, then circling around the outside of it.

One day the company engineer decided to drive to Joffre Falls and invited me and another student to go with him. His car was a Morris Minor but he got there!

It was the end of the dry season, so water was not flowing. It would be spectacular when it was!

There was a lot of water in some sections of the gorge, so we couldn't go too far.

Not too far in, we saw a snake on a rock ledge. It was an unusual colour and shape with a short, fat body and a skinny tail.

From the shape of its body, it didn't look as if it could move very fast, so I moved in quite close to take a photo. Later when I showed the photo to locals they told me it was a death adder and very dangerous. They told me the snake would cover itself with sand leaving only the skinny tail exposed. Then it would wriggle its tail to attract its next victim.

On the way back we stopped at the local pub for a few drinks.

The word went out – rain was on the way!

At first it was just a few heavy drops, quickly absorbed by the dry, red earth. But then the drops increased in number until it became a steady downpour. The colour of the earth grew darker, and puddles formed.

Early Wittenoom Gorge

Death Adder

Wittenoom Hotel

Upstream, the puddles joined together to form creeks. One of the largest creeks found its way to Joffre Falls and filled each step to the bottom. The creek then started to pour into the beginning of Wittenoom Gorge, flushing out the pools of water left from last year!

The creek would find its way to the power station, then to the top end of the company's housing. It would sweep around the housing area, following the gorge.

We grew impatient and ran to the top end of the housing area and waited. At first there was only a trickle of water but it soon grew to a steady flow. We ran to the other end of the housing area just in time to see a steady flow of water racing towards the sea, hundreds of kilometres away. We followed it far enough to see our waterhole being flushed out.

I will always miss the peace and quiet and the long walks around Wittenoom Gorge, just as I avoid crowded, noisy places.

KANGAROO ISLAND

In 1991 the Seven Network introduced a new program called "The Main Event".

The highlight of the show was a quiz competition between two families. The families were in different states and the whole show was live.

A Subaru car was the prize for the winning family.

South Australian families had won six times in a row!

Now the producers selected a family (who had applied) from Kangaroo Island.

Before they could go ahead with it, we had to confirm it was possible to get live pictures from Kangaroo Island to Sydney and back. That meant we had to see if we could get a link signal from Kangaroo Island to Mount Lofty and back.

To find out, the director, Greg Packer, and I had to go to Kangaroo Island. We made an early start heading for Cape

Jervis in the Hiace van with some link equipment. We drove down South Road through Mount Compass and took the turnoff to Victor Harbor. I was almost at Victor Harbor before I realised I shouldn't have taken that turn!

Luckily there is a good road from Victor Harbor to Cape Jervis, so we didn't lose too much time.

> "Transmitting microwave signals over water with the Earth's curvature can have its own problems.

When we arrived at Cape Jervis we registered the Hiace van and joined the queue of vehicles waiting to load onto the ferry. After arriving at Kangaroo Island we headed towards Kingscote. Consulting our maps and the address we were given, we found the turnoff before we reached Kingscote. As we drove further south into the bush it became obvious that we would not be able to get a link path out. When we arrived at the farm, they told us they had been given approval to use an alternative location at a relative's house in Kingscote.

We drove back to Kingscote and followed the directions. The house was on the outskirts of Kingscote, near the top of some high cliffs looking north, there was a clear view across Gulf St. Vincent to Mount Lofty and our Station Transmitter tower.

This was the best possible location from Kangaroo Island!

The only question now was whether our links could handle the distance over water.

Transmitting microwave signals over water with the Earth's curvature can have its own problems. I set up a two foot diameter link dish on a tripod and connected a 2 GHz link transmitter with a 10 watt amp to the dish. They were powered with battery packs. A colour bar generator fed into the link transmitter, completed the test setup.

I adjusted the dish, so it was pointing towards Mount Lofty and switched on the link transmitter. I then called Master Control and asked them to look for our signal.

Master Control adjusted the receiver dish at Mount Lofty for maximum signal strength, then I adjusted the dish at my end to increase signal level to a peak. The result was quite useable and Master Control recorded our colour bars for confirmation.

> ”
> The main problem occurs at sunset, when changes in air temperature can bend or deflect the signal like a mirage.

We packed up the equipment and headed for the ferry and home. It was a good result for the day. However we didn't have a Backup Link or a return link and I was concerned about a link path over water.

The next day I rang Sam Watts, the Network expert in microwave equipment, to ask his opinion. He said he had a four foot dish for a 2 GHz link, which would increase signal level significantly. He also warned me that a long link path over water could cause problems.

The main problem occurs at sunset, when changes in air temperature can bend or deflect the signal like a mirage. It was better to just wait for the signal to stabilise. Don't try to chase it! The next problem was the backup link. A 7 GHz link with four foot dishes at each end would result in noisy pictures but the risk was worth it for the novelty and publicity of the location.

> "The return link was essential for the family quiz part of the show.

The return link was essential for the family quiz part of the show. This was a video and audio feed from the Sydney studios to the contestants' home on Kangaroo Island.

The first section of this was by Fibre from Sydney to SAS Studio in Adelaide. Next was a permanent studio transmitter link from SAS Studio to the Mount Lofty Transmitter building.

The final stage of the return link was exactly the reverse to the one just tested. To achieve this we hired the ADS Channel 10 link van. The link van had a 2 GHz link with a 10 watt amplifier, which was connected to a two foot antenna on a ten metre telescopic mast!

With the link van parked next to the Channel 7 Transmitter tower we could achieve the same link path as the test – but in reverse.

Now that the links had been arranged, I could look after some other details. I arranged for E.T.S.A. to connect a three phase power box to the Stobie pole outside the house at Kingscote. Meanwhile, Operations organised a four wire communications order wire at the house, to be connected by Telecom.

I made up a list of equipment to be loaded on the support truck. It was a long way back to the Station if we forgot something! The vehicles needed a full tank of fuel for the trip, and battery packs had to be fully charged.

Just before we were about to leave I was handed some cash. Twenty dollars per diem for each member of the crew. I was told not to just hand out a twenty dollar note to each person. Instead, I should use the cash I had been given to pay for any food or drinks that the crew wanted.

That seemed strange, and I couldn't see how it could work. But I would give it a try!

We arrived at Cape Jervis in good time and loaded onto the ferry. The weather was mild and the sea fairly calm, but as we got further out there were some large waves making the vehicles rock in time.

The Mercedes OB van was rocking more than the others because it was top heavy and had a soft suspension.

I became seriously concerned it might roll over.

We had a few strong ropes, so I tied one end of the ropes to a railing around the roof of the van. The other ends I tied off to solid rails or fittings on the ferry. It seemed to stabilise the van.

After driving the vehicles off the ferry the crew immediately went to a shop to stock up on food and drinks. I asked the shopkeeper to tally up what the crew bought and I would pay for it. I had no idea how much each individual had spent.

This was not going to work!

We drove straight to the house and began setting up equipment. While the others set up cameras, lights, monitors, and ran cables, I concentrated on the links. Three link dishes were set up on the roof of the OB van, then the link transmitters and link receivers were connected to the appropriate dishes. Finally, video, audio and power cables were connected. A three phase power cable was strung up from the Stobie pole to the roof of the van.

"We all sat anxiously watching the return link for any sign of change.

After checking the connections and voltages we connected power to the van and switched on equipment. I turned on the links and rang Master Control. We began the job of adjusting the pan and tilt controls of each dish to peak the signal strength on each receiver. The results were what we had expected.

We all began to relax a little!

Greg was inside talking to the family, explaining what to do. He also told them because the location was so different and because the family lived on a farm, Subaru had agreed to increase the prize from a small car to a Subaru 4WD!

The crew had gathered around the OB van and were taking orders for a meal. I decided I couldn't handle the per diem payments the way I had been asked, so I handed each member of the crew a twenty dollar note. They were all very happy at the extra payment and I was out of pocket!

By late afternoon it was already starting to cool down. The picture on the return link was still clean and signal level hadn't changed. By 5.30 pm the sun was sitting on the horizon. We all sat anxiously watching the return link for any sign of change.

Master Control called to tell us that the 7 GHz backup link had died. There was no sign of a picture!

I reminded them not to touch the pan and tilt controls. A few minutes later the picture on the return link disappeared. Replaced with noise. I called Master Control to let them know. As I was speaking the main link went to noise.

All we could do was wait, while looking at a screen of noise!

Nobody said a word, but as each minute passed I could feel the tension rising. After half an hour had passed, people started to question whether we should start adjusting the dish for the return link and see where the signal had gone.

I decided I could mark the current pan and tilt positions and return to the same position later. That couldn't harm anything, and it would feel like I was doing something useful.

"All we could do was wait, while looking at a screen of noise!

Before I could do anything, Master Control called to say our main link had returned but it was very noisy. It would require some adjustment. Within minutes the return link had returned with a very noisy picture, so the crew moved back to their working positions ready for the show.

Master Control called to tell me that they hadn't been able to improve the signal level on the main link and it was still noisy. It must be on a side lobe. The dishes focus the signal to a central peak surrounded by a series of smaller peaks or side lobes.

I asked Master Control to pan and tilt the dish at their end over a wide range to see if they could pick up the central peak. After several minutes they called back to say they couldn't find any central peak.

I started to pan the four foot dish for the 2 GHz transmitter while Master Control read out the signal strength on the receiver. We found a few smaller peaks but not the main one. Then I moved the tilt control down, but only one small peak there.

"

A couple of small peaks appeared then the signal level shot up. We had found the main peak!

All that was left was to tilt up.

A couple of small peaks appeared then the signal level shot up. We had found the main peak!

After a few minor adjustments to the main link we turned to the return link. Since tilting the dish on the main link fixed the problem, we tried the same for the return link with immediate success. The backup link would not be needed.

Relief showed on people's faces as they relaxed.

Our Kangaroo Island family performed well and won the Subaru 4WD vehicle! That was the seventh win in a row for South Australia. As a "thank you" the family brought out some celebratory food and drinks for the crew!

Then it was time to pack up the equipment and head for the hotel in Kingscote for the night.

Next morning we drove across to Penneshaw to put the vehicles on the ferry. Once again I tied ropes from the roof of the OB van to anchor points on the ferry. I could see the ropes straining as we crossed Backstairs Passage.

While watching the OB van, Suzanne, the makeup artist, approached and said, "The rest of the crew got twenty dollars each, why didn't I get one?"

She wasn't present when I handed out the twenty-dollar notes. I apologised profusely and took twenty dollars from my wallet and gave it to her. She said, "Thanks!" – but didn't seem too happy.

I think she felt it was some kind of discrimination.

I'm sure I was seriously out of pocket.

Years later, thinking back to this day, I wondered if Makeup was a freelance job, and if it was, was she entitled to per diem payment?

It was my own fault for not keeping records! However, I did have a lot of other things to think about!

The OB was successful and the family won a car!

MISSING SWITCHES

When Australian television switched to colour in 1975 the television stations had to replace most of their equipment – including Outside Broadcast vans.

Most stations decided larger vans would be required in the future and so most bought semi-trailer vans for their main production unit.

At SAS, the director of engineering, Peter Smith, decided OB vans would be smaller and so, without any discussion with anyone with experience in that area, he ordered a Mercedes camper van to build an OB van.

He argued that equipment was getting smaller and so OB vans should be smaller. I said that people were not getting smaller. In fact, people were getting bigger, and producers and directors would want more facilities!

The Mercedes camper van would only be big enough for three colour cameras. Peter Smith said, "There will never be more than three cameras on an Outside Broadcast in Adelaide."

I did the best I could with the vehicle we were given.

A few years later, for regular telecasts of basketball at the Apollo Stadium, we used seven cameras!

The Adelaide Crows joined the AFL in 1991. As a Seven Network station we had the rights to cover AFL matches at Football Park – but our OB van was inadequate.

HSV Channel 7 Melbourne said they had an OB van we could use for AFL matches. Greg Packer and I flew to Melbourne to look at it. That was a waste of time. The van was smaller than the Mercedes and in poor condition with fewer facilities. They obviously had some ulterior motive in offering it!

We had to hire Channel 9's van for three years at Football Park until the embarrassment became too much. It was then the Sydney Management decided something had to be done!

I had prepared a proposal to build an OB van in Adelaide with layout and drawings based on HSV Channel 7 Melbourne's van. A Sydney executive came to Adelaide to study the proposal and took copies back to Sydney.

The Sydney Management decided they would rather spend the money on a new Studio Control Room in Sydney and give us one of their OB vans. They had three OB vans, MPU (Mobile Production Unit), OB 1 and OB 2.

Guess which one they sent to Adelaide?

Sydney's OB 2 van had to be upgraded to meet the AFL requirements, particularly in audio and talkback. ATN Channel 7's technician, Kevin Riley, drove OB 2 to Adelaide and stayed in Adelaide for several days to explain details of cables, patching, talkback etc.

He mentioned that the ROSS, a Canadian-made vision mixing desk, had a "small problem". Sydney techs hadn't been able to find the cause of the problem or how to fix it. He said he couldn't remember what the problem was, but he would let me know when he remembered. He never did let me know but eventually I found out!

> "If two buttons were pressed at the same time, only the lower numbered one would work, preventing the higher numbered switch from operating.

In his second season directing football from OB 2, the director, Greg Packer, came to me after a match and said sometimes when he pushed a camera input button on the ROSS, it wouldn't switch! I asked which button? Greg said it was mostly CAM 2 but he thought sometimes it also happened on CAM 4.

The following week I powered up the van and began switching on the PGM row of the ROSS desk. After about 15 minutes continuous switching, up and down the PGM row, it hadn't failed. Looking at the circuits for the desk, I found there was interlock wiring through groups of switches, this would prevent two switches occurring at the same time.

If two buttons were pressed at the same time, only the lower numbered one would work, preventing the higher numbered switch from operating.

It was wired-up in such a way, that if you pressed one button, say CAM 4, but accidentally caught the edge of the previous button, CAM 3, and carried it half-way down, then neither switch would work. (The switches were "break before make").

I explained this to Greg and demonstrated it to him, to see if that was the problem.

> I was convinced the problem was in the software not the hardware.

However, after the next AFL match Greg said several switches failed and he was sure that he had only pushed one button. The following week, once again I powered up the van and began switching up and down the PGM row of the ROSS switcher.

Again, I was just about ready to give up, when a switch failed. It wasn't CAM 2 or CAM 4, so I continued switching – with a bit more attention!

After a few hours continuous switching I found:

1. It wasn't just the PGM row but any row of the desk.
2. The failed switches were completely random.
3. The failure rate was about one switch in 200 to 300!

I sent a fax to ROSS in Canada explaining the problem. I asked if they had similar problems or could suggest any solution.

They sent a fax back saying in their opinion the problem was caused by faulty switches. They had experienced problems with these switches. But I was convinced the problem was in the software not the hardware.

The switches are organised into rows and columns, then scanned by a keyboard scanner chip. It was a keyboard scanner commonly used in computer keyboards. I tried replacing the keyboard scanner chip but there was no change.

A Z80 microprocessor reads out the switch information from the keyboard scanner and processes it. A group of us had been to a TAFE course on the Z80, so I was reasonably familiar with the Z80, but not some of the other chips involved.

I asked the head technician, Ken Webster, if there was anyone in Maintenance who might be able to help me and he nominated Walter Long. So Walter went to the OB van to see what the problem was. After about 30 minutes Walter walked off saying that he didn't have time for this and he had three other jobs to do!

On my own again! I sent another fax to ROSS asking for any details on the software program for their vision mixer. In the meantime, we had a football match to cover in Melbourne.

Because the Crows had half their games at home and half away, fifty per cent of our weekends we had no game at Football Park. However, Melbourne could have up to four games in a weekend, so it was organised we would cover one game for them.

I would drive the OB van and Steve Stevens would drive the support truck with cameras, lenses, tripods and other items. On Thursday we would load the equipment in the vehicles ready for an early start on Friday. Then on Friday we would drive the vehicles to Melbourne. The rest would unfold like this:

- Saturday we would cover a football match with a Melbourne crew
- Sunday drive back to Adelaide.
- Monday we would unpack, clean, fix, and recharge equipment.
- Tuesday and Wednesday off.

On one such trip, at the end of the match, the Melbourne director came to me to complain that sometimes, when he pushed a button it didn't switch. It seemed strange it took Greg Packer two seasons to realise it was the vision mixer that was faulty, not his switching. Somehow this Melbourne director knew the first time in this van.

I suspect that Greg tipped him off to stir things up!

I explained it was a software problem and I was waiting for a reply from ROSS in Canada with some information. He said, "You should leave the van in Melbourne. We've got some pretty good techs in Melbourne. They will fix it for you." I said I didn't think I could just leave the van in Melbourne but I would pass on his concerns to our head technician.

On Sunday we drove the vehicles back to Adelaide. By the time I got to work on Monday (it was a 10.30 am start) I found that the Melbourne director had complained about the ROSS switcher to Melbourne's operations manager. He rang the SAS operations manager, who passed it on to Ken, our head technician.

Ken asked Walter why he hadn't fixed it. In the end, Ken said that he would fix it. He took some equipment to the OB van and began work.

I had Tuesday and Wednesday off. When I came in on Thursday I found Ken had spent three days in the van without success. Unfortunately a vital component in the ROSS desk was damaged in the process and a replacement could not be obtained locally.

A replacement would have to come from ROSS in Canada and would take several days. To make things worse the OB van was booked to go back to Melbourne the next day! The replacement part arrived a few days later and was installed in the vision mixer.

The head technician said that he couldn't afford to spend any more time on it and besides it was Sydney's van so they should fix it! A fax came back from ROSS in reply to my request for more information. They said that they could not give me any more information because of software security concerns.

On my own again! I had a book with the Z80 Instruction Codes, so I started decoding the program. My next two days' off were cold and wet. It didn't stop raining, so I stoked up the combustion heater at home and spent the next two days decoding the Z80 program.

With the decoded program and a Logic Analyser, the missing switches were tracked down. They were being sent to the wrong place and the problem could easily be fixed by changing one byte.

I showed Walter the results with the decoded notes and logic analyser. He said, "I'll get Ken. Show him." So I repeated the explanation to Ken. He picked up the bundle of foolscap pages with the decoded notes and said, "You can't have much to do if you had time to do all this."

I didn't tell him that I did most of it at home!

Tortoise and the Hare?

RAMBLINGS OF AN OB SUPERVISOR

I said goodbye to the dog and cat, then paused for a minute to watch the horses wandering around the paddock … didn't have time to call them up and give them an apple each!

They had already eaten all the lower apples from the trees in the bottom paddock.

Driving the station wagon down the dirt road at the bottom of Germantown Hill an African daisy caught my eye. I would have to get rid of it over the weekend.

There was always something to do!

In a few years' time I could be looking at retirement. There wouldn't be enough work for two OB supervisors at Channel 7.

In less than a minute I was on the freeway, and in thirty minutes I was at the Station. Letting myself in through the hatch in the garage door and stepping into the gloom of the darkened garage was like stepping into another world.

I shouldn't complain, I always thought that OB Supervisor was the best job in television.

There was a lot of variety in both work and equipment … the OB van was a television station on wheels, separate from the politics and hassles of the rest of the Station!

But there were some who would have liked to take that from me by any means.

I switched on the garage lights, and it seemed a little more friendly. Then the phone rang. It was a journo from the Newsroom. They wanted to make some arrangements for a Live Cross in the news that night. That seemed strange. Usually they left those things till three or four o'clock in the afternoon.

Then he said that we would need to use the SNG unit (Satellite News Gathering).

One of the advantages of the SNG is that it can be used in remote locations or outside the range of microwave links.

If the Newsroom wanted a live news cross from a remote location it would make sense to get an early start. I asked where the cross was to be from. He said they didn't have an exact location but it would be to the north of the city, and they wanted to be first there. "Get a good position, front and centre," he said. I quickly checked the SNG, made sure the generator had fuel and the battery-powered Spectrum Analyser was charged up. Of course they were. Bill would have done that! I hitched the trailer on to the back of a four-wheel drive and started heading north.

Back on the open road again felt good. Driving away from the city with paddocks on both sides of the road was relaxing. I

SNG in operation

began to think about retirement and our finances. I would miss some of the work and some of the people I worked with. But there are some I would never miss.

A car going in the opposite direction with its lights on reminded me of one example. We were setting up for an Outside Broadcast when a member of the floor crew warned me that the troublemaker had deliberately turned on the headlights of the OB van.

Because it was daylight and because of the way I had parked the van I probably wouldn't have seen the headlights!

By the end of the OB the battery would have been flat and I would get the blame and seem incompetent. That was typical tactics.

If you can't show that you are better than someone else, then make them appear worse by repeated mistakes!

Fortunately the two department heads I report to are well aware of who the troublemakers are.

I was brought back to the present by the ringing of my phone. It was the Newsroom again. They had just received details of the location for the Live Cross.

They wanted me to set up outside an old unused bank building in Snowtown.

"Bloody Newsroom," I muttered. "What could possibly happen in Snowtown that's so important. Maybe a sheep with two heads?"

But I still didn't know what the story was, so I kept driving north until I reached the turnoff to Snowtown.

How was I supposed to know which building was the old bank building? It would probably be in the main street. I turned into the main street and didn't have any trouble identifying the building.

It would be the building with two police cars parked outside and two cops standing guard at the entrance. One of the cops spotted the satellite dish then nudged his partner, and they both watched me drive down the street.

I was told, "front and centre," but the police had that spot.

The next best spot was across the road. Probably a better position anyway. A wide-shot would show the whole building and the police.

I pulled into two parking bays directly opposite them.

Fortunately the road ran north-south, with the back of the trailer pointing north.

The back of the trailer must face approximately north because the dish has a limited range of movement and the satellite is over the equator, in a line of height somewhere between Sydney and Melbourne. I separated the trailer from the four-wheel drive and let the air out of the airbag suspension to lower the trailer onto its stops.

Bill said to do that!

One time I forgot to let the airbags down. After a while the air leaked out and the airbags slowly went down. The dish started to tilt down and the picture became noisy.

With the trailer firmly on its stops, I used a winch (which Bill had installed) to lift the generator off the trailer and onto a trolley. The winch made it a one-man operation. Then I released the screws which held the dish in place for transport and began scanning the sky for the satellite.

The battery-powered spectrum analyser soon picked up a satellite, but there were three satellites in that part of the sky!

Each satellite generates its own pattern of signals. This meant I could pick out the right one and then make a phone call to check the polarity of the dish. All signals are polarised vertically or horizontally and any error could cause interference to an adjacent user.

Finally I could set the frequency and check test signals to Master Control. Having set it all up I shut it all down again and switched off the generator. Nothing to do now for the next six hours but wait, and I didn't even know what the story was about!

> ” The battery-powered spectrum analyser soon picked up a satellite, but there were three satellites in that part of the sky!

I could ask one of the cops.

"Just happened to be passing with my satellite dish to see what's happening."

Don't think so!

Just then a car from one of the radio stations arrived, so I asked the driver what he knew. He said several people had been murdered and their bodies stuffed into barrels and stored in the bank.

A large deposit? The jokes would come, mostly in poor taste.

The media continued to arrive – newspaper journalists, photographers, radio and television representatives. Channel 2 and Channel 10 arrived at almost the same time. They looked around, then recorded a piece to camera but could not see any value in staying.

Channel 9 arrived in two vehicles. The first vehicle was a standard news car. The second vehicle was a dual-cab covered ute – a Channel 9 OB work vehicle.

The driver got out. It was Wayne, the Channel 9 OB supervisor, a very experienced hard-working tech. He was carrying a pair of binoculars and looking to the south. He was going to try to get a link path back to Mount Lofty. It would require a repeater site on the way. The only possible place for a repeater was on the Hummocks.

"Everyone had trouble with their mobile phones, and the more people arrived the worse it got!

Finding a repeater site on the Hummocks and setting up a double-hop over the distances in only six hours, would be near impossible!

Wayne got back in his ute and headed south. My phone rang. It was the Newsroom. After only a few seconds it dropped out. There wasn't a mobile phone tower in Snowtown.

Later a local claimed that the nearest phone tower was in Port Pirie!

Everyone had trouble with their mobile phones, and the more people arrived the worse it got!

I wandered around checking reception and found a few better spots. The Newsroom rang back and told me that they were going to host the whole news service from Snowtown.

Walking and talking on the phone reminded me of a call I received at home one night. When I answered the phone, a drunken voice sang the Humphrey Bear song: "What a funny old fellow is Humphrey …" I couldn't recognise the voice, but I knew who they were!

It was a small clique of bullies who seemed to derive pleasure in harassing people. One in particular had baited me several times, trying to provoke me into a physical confrontation. I think he fancied himself!

A news crew arrived to assess the situation and record some background vision. Our working area was clearly marked out with cables and a few items of equipment. Wayne from Channel 9 returned with a link transmitter and started to set it up.

I walked over to say hello. He told me they were planning several live crosses during their news. Wayne was confident they would have a double-hop link path back to Mt. Lofty. He said they had a contact who knew the owner of a property on the Hummocks.

More people kept arriving, a lot of them were locals, just there out of curiosity. It was getting to be more like Rundle Street.

A few of our crew started to turn up. There was a Floor Manager, Lighting, Audio, Makeup and the Workshop crew with props. Finally the newsreader, Jane Doyle, arrived. I started the generator to check lighting and then kept out of the way.

After a few minutes I saw Jane heading in my direction.

She said, “Mike, my phone keeps dropping out, and I have to check out my scripts with the Studio. Is there anything that can be done to fix it?”

“ The satellite phone was a fairly early model and came in a briefcase with an external antenna.

There’s not much good having a satellite dish to send vision and sound from a remote location if you haven’t got communications to know when, where, how and so on, to send it!

So the SNG has a satellite phone. “Thanks Bill!”

I set up the satellite phone and gave Jane a brief explanation on how to use it.

The satellite phone was a fairly early model and came in a briefcase with an external antenna.

It was only a few minutes before the journalist complained that they had to phone through the story but their phone kept dropping out. Is there anything I could do to help?

The four-wheel drive had a car phone fitted in it with an external aerial. The external aerial gave it enough extra gain so it didn’t drop out.

That left me with my basic mobile phone. The phone rang as I was heading for one of the locations where the mobile phone signal strength was better. As I answered the phone a voice said, “This is ATN Sydney ....” The phone dropped out.

A few seconds later they called back. “Is that Mike Humphry?”

I said, “Yes.”

"Mike, this is ATN Master Control, we would like to …"

I waited for him to call back again and then said, "Phone reception is terrible here. You're going to have to work directly with our Master Control."

He didn't like that!

I had struck this a few times before. They don't like to work with our Newsroom where the attitude is, "It's our story, in our area, and we control it."

Sydney claimed to be the number one Station in the Network (Melbourne would disagree with that), so Sydney wanted control of any major event or news story. If necessary, through the back door!

I switched on the SNG to give us one more means of communication. The Newsroom had control of the satellite phone and the car phone. Now they had IFB (Interrupted Foldback).

The satellite booking included a video and audio channel from the remote location to the satellite and a return audio feed from the satellite to the remote location.

The IFB sound is fed to the journalist's or newsreader's earpiece as well as to the cameraman, and, in this case, the floor manager.

The foldback sound comes from selected audio sources from the Studio, fed back to the SNG and interrupted by any cues or instructions from the producer or director.

The crew was getting ready for final checks … Jane sat on a stool, in position … Lights were adjusted … Jane polished her glasses one final time as Makeup did a final check.

The news producer called for a check on the IFB and the crew confirmed they could hear it.

As the crew tested and confirmed everything was working as expected, I could see Wayne starting a generator. Their journalist was looking agitated as Wayne hurried to switch on and check various pieces of equipment.

At six o'clock both Stations went to air with their lead story crossing to Snowtown. Our crosses were polished and professional. Channel 9's were also professional, but without the facilities it couldn't match Channel 7!

Would viewers at home really switch between channels and notice the difference?

Channel 9 finished first and began to pack up their equipment. Their cameraman crossed close behind me as he walked to his car. He was talking on his phone complaining about technical delays when he stopped abruptly. His phone had dropped out!

A few minutes later we finished our last cross into the news. Jane went to each person in the crew and thanked them for their effort.

You don't get to the top without the support of the crew behind you!

The crew then packed up the equipment they were responsible for, and then one by one, they headed for home. I packed up all of the SNG equipment, returned the dish to its travel position and locked it down.

When I shut down the generator it was suddenly quiet and dark. After loading the generator on to the trailer and connecting the trailer to the four-wheel drive vehicle, I drove out of Snowtown heading for Adelaide.

The last one to leave!

There was little traffic on the road. A good time to relax and think about the events of the day. Several murderers had been locked up, and the News Department had presented a full news service by satellite.

They would be celebrating in the Newsroom, congratulating Jane on her performance. But there would be no mention of the person who contributed most to the program – Bill Rowse!

> " You don't get to the top without the support of the crew behind you!

Bill provided the SNG with a satellite phone and IFB, making life very easy for me.

As I drove past the Hummocks I wondered if Wayne had finished packing up the repeater site. The Channel 9 Newsroom might also be celebrating, but I doubt whether Wayne would get the credit he deserved!

He had done what I thought was almost impossible.

Both Wayne and Bill made it possible for their respective Stations to cross live to Snowtown.

The locals would resent the notoriety!

Would the viewers realise the time, effort and skill that went into this news report?

Would Wayne have anyone challenging him for his job?

I had one such person and he eventually gave up, but he still maintained the same attitude!

It must have eaten away at him. I had the job he wanted, and I suspect the lifestyle as well.

In addition it must have really hurt when I was sent to Japan for the Hitachi camera acceptance test! His attitude had been going on for years!

After a while I learnt to ignore him.

When I left the Station I would switch … OFF!!

TIME OUT

Portable cameras are an important part of sporting events … and cable trackers are an important element!

A cable tracker is a person who picks up the slack in the cable when there is an excess and feeds it out when required.

Very often when a cameraman moves back and forth along a boundary, he will tend to keep turning in the same direction, which means the cable becomes twisted.

At every opportunity he will try to untwist the cable by turning the camera around in the opposite direction.

For major sporting events like golf or the tennis at the Australian Open, enormous facilities are needed, so the Network pools their resources. Cables and equipment are requested from each Station in the Network. For a Golf OB in Melbourne they asked us to supply a particular zoom lens we had.

I was asked to pack it up and send it off. When I looked for the lens it was missing. After asking a number of people if they knew where it was, I was told a cameraman, Andy Arragant, had borrowed the lens and driven to Middleton Beach on the south coast to record some surfing shots.

I had to call Melbourne and tell them the lens would be a day late.

Arragant was reprimanded and told not to take equipment without permission. He took no notice.

When it was decided to cover the basketball, our OB van was only built for three cameras. In a short space of time this was increased to seven cameras.

Audio requirements had also increased – with stereo sound and effects needed.

To cope with the extra facilities, a transportable shed was hired and fitted out as an Audio Control Room. This created some extra space in the OB van and four more camera monitors were fitted over the audio desk.

The Apollo Stadium was always packed, and audience seating was very close to the side of the court. This left only a narrow walkway for audience access to toilets and to the food or drinks shops. The audience shared this narrow space with the cameraman and cable tracker who continually moved from one end of the court to the other.

It always seemed a little risky having a portable camera trailing a cable in a confined space with the general public.

The cameraman, Glen Rickard, seemed to be aware of the risk and took care of his movements. But the director, Geoff Dickson, wanted more action from the camera and gave the portable camera to Arragant with Glen Rickard as cable tracker.

Arragant immediately began running flat out from one end of the court to the other. I told him to slow down, stop running, but he ignored me! I then asked Geoff to tell Arragant to stop running. He made a half-hearted effort saying, "Yeah, better slow down a bit Andy."

This brought no response, so I told Geoff I would shut down that camera if he didn't stop running!

He said, "OK, Andy, better stop running!" This had the desired effect and he slowed down to a fast walk. A few minutes later he was running again

I disconnected the camera and told Geoff I wanted to see Andy at the back of the stadium.

There is an area under the stadium seating where we run cables. Arragant and Glen were waiting for me when I arrived. He immediately pointed the camera at me, with the lens only inches from my face. I pushed the lens away and said, "Give the camera to Glen."

At first he didn't move, so I said, "If you don't give the camera to Glen, I will disconnect it for the rest of the night."

Geoff was obviously listening through the talkback and must have instructed Arragant to hand over the camera.

There were no more problems that night, but I was sure there would be repercussions on Monday morning!

As predicted I was invited to a meeting in the boardroom first thing Monday morning.

I arrived at the appointed time. Geoff Dickson was already there. We didn't speak.

Then Senior Director Al Sylvesta arrived, looking very smug and confident with a puffed-up chest. He sat down.

Just the three of us.

Al said, "I believe we had a problem at the basketball on Saturday night?"

Geoff chipped in, "Yes, Mike disconnected one of our cameras and demanded that we change one of the cameramen."

I said, "After three warnings were ignored."

Al said, "Don't you think that was a bit heavy handed?"

"No! The only way to get Arragant to do what he was told was to take him off camera."

"You don't have the authority!" said Al, the volume increasing with each word to shout 'authority'.

I wasn't going to try to match Al in volume.

In a quiet, calm, rehearsed voice I said, "I'm on the Health and Safety Committee, and I have every right to check on the safety of the crew and the general public. If I find that something is potentially dangerous to either, I will take whatever action is needed."

Al was not prepared for this answer, "Is this true, Geoff?"

Geoff said, "We've got a cable tracker."

I said, "You could have half a dozen cable trackers and you still couldn't guarantee that no-one would trip over the cable.

"You had a cameraman and cable tracker running flat out, trailing a cable in a narrow, shared space!

"That's the definition of stupidity. If I got a Government Safety Inspector to look at the situation, he would take one look and say, 'no cameras to be in the shared space'."

If the Health and Safety Committee made a formal report a copy would be sent to Management.

Al was smart enough to know that would be the end of it.

The meeting ended abruptly with an assurance there would be no more running in a space shared with the general public.

SHOCKING CAMERAS

When a Melbourne cameraman received a serious electric shock from a portable Hitachi camera, it sent alarm bells ringing!

The camera has a complicated protection system. Something must have overcome the system.

This would involve the triax cable and connectors.

The triax cable has three conductors:

1. The centre conductor is a single wire down the middle of the cable.
2. The inner shield is a cylindrical mesh surrounding the centre conductor.
3. The outer shield is a cylindrical mesh surrounding the inner shield.

The three conductors are separated by insulation material.

When a camera is connected to a Camera Control Unit (CCU) by triax cable, the outer shield connects to the frame of the CCU which gives the outer shield a solid EARTH. The other end of the outer shield connects to the frame of the camera which EARTHs the camera.

Inside the camera, a link connects the outer shield to the inner shield, so that the inner shield returns to the CCU at EARTH potential. This creates an EARTH LOOP from the CCU to the camera and back to the CCU.

The integrity of the EARTH LOOP is tested by a single transistor circuit connected to the inner shield. If the EARTH LOOP is intact, the protection system gives a green light to switch camera power from standby (safe) to operate.

If there is a break in the EARTH LOOP the protection system gives a red light, forcing camera power to stay at standby mode. A red light here also tells a microprocessor to put the message "CABLE OPEN" on the CCU monitor.

A "CABLE OPEN" message could mean one of three things:

1. A break in the outer shield.
2. A break in the inner shield.
3. Removal of the link in the camera. (Ninety-nine per cent of the time it's because the cable is not plugged into the camera.)

Camera power must be switched to standby if a cable is unplugged from a camera!

To be sure of this, the camera has a backup protection system.

The backup protection system involves the camera intercom system.

The camera intercom is powered by either 'standby' power or 'operate' power. When turned on, the camera intercom sends a radio frequency signal down the triax.

If the CCU detects this signal there must be a camera attached to the triax.

No signal means no camera on the triax.

This information is passed on to the microprocessor to be combined with the main protection system.

Whenever our cables go to Sydney or Melbourne for a Golf OB, I check them on return.

On one occasion a cable came back with a short between the inner and outer shields. To check the effect on a camera, I plugged it into a CCU. The message on the monitor changed from "CABLE OPEN" to "INCOM LINE NG".

I had seen that message many times before on Golf OBs and at Football Park.

To track it down, I measured the resistance of the cable from each end to the short. I then calculated approximately where the short should be. I then carefully examined the cable. There was a puncture mark on the outer cover!

Cutting away a small square of the outer cover to expose the outer shield, I could clearly see that whatever punctured the cable had caught some of the braid and pushed it through to the inner shield causing a short!

Was it an accident or deliberate?

Then I remembered!

GOLF SHOES!!

Golf shoes with sprigs!

A portable camera

So what effect will this have on the protection system? A short between the shields provides an alternative EARTH LOOP – up the outer shield, through the short, and down the inner shield.

> “
> That would send about 300 volts AC to the camera with no return path, except through the cameraman, down to ground!

Meanwhile anything could happen at the other end of the cable and the protection system wouldn't know about it!

The outer shield could be broken, or the inner shield, or both, but the protection system sees an unbroken EARTH LOOP and gives a green light to stay on operate mode.

That would send about 300 volts AC to the camera with no return path, except through the cameraman, down to ground!

Only the backup protection system could stop it. This would depend on a number of factors.

If a triax cable that is plugged into a CCU has a short between the shields and no camera attached, then the protection system will see an EARTH LOOP and believe that a camera is attached! But the backup protection system can detect no RF signal, creating a conflict.

If the main protection system sees a camera, but the backup system can't, maybe there is a problem with the intercom!

If so, the CCU Monitor displays “INCOM LINE NG”.

It seemed to be an Engineering problem, so I wrote a report and sent it to the chief engineer.

Might as well have sent it to a black hole!

I should have sent copies to HSV Channel 7 in Melbourne.

P.S. How does a break occur in an inner shield?

In a triax connector, the contact for the inner shield is a cylinder. In the male connector it is a solid cylinder and in the female connector the cylinder is split into six segments. In joining the two connectors, the six segments slide over the solid cylinder and act as spring contacts absorbing any movement.

After a few years use the Hitachi Portable (F3) cameras started to shut down with some movements of the camera. There was some doubt whether it was the centre pin or the inner shield breaking contact, but the monitor gave the message "CABLE OPEN". That means the EARTH LOOP is open and not the centre pin.

A careful examination of the triax socket on the camera shows that the segments of the inner shield have spread, so if the two connectors are in line, there is a gap between them.

A temporary fix is to use a small screwdriver to carefully lever the segments back to their normal position.

P.P.S. How do you fix a short between the shields?

When a golf shoe sprig penetrates a cable it sometimes snags a few strands of the outer shield and pushes it through to the inner shield causing a short.

In most cases it should only take one or two strands of fine mesh wire. By passing a heavy current through the short it may be possible to destroy it like a fuse.

Just a suggestion: I've never tried it!

P.P.P.S. When is an open outer shield not open?

Some triax cables had cuts in the outer cover and were then left lying in salt water at a Birdman Rally OB at Glenelg.

Years later the outer shield became brittle and shredded with a resistance of megohms per metre.

Might as well be open!

CHANGES

Alcohol could be a problem on OBs – particularly at the Hilton Hotel and the Convention Centre where the crew could convince the waiters and waitresses to keep them supplied with drinks!

After one OB at the Hilton Hotel I asked some of the crew to help me de-rig and carry the links to the tender truck. The links were on the roof of the hotel.

While I was dismantling one of the links I noticed a cameraman staggering around the roof saying, "Look at all the city lights!"

There was no safety rail around the roof. If he stepped off the edge it was an eighty to ninety metre drop to the ground.

After that incident, at production meetings I would always bring up the subject of drinking during an OB. That had no effect on a few feral members of the crew!

At a Golf OB, Trevor Lanyon arrived with a large esky full of ice-cold beer. The esky was sealed with masking tape, not to be opened until pack up complete.

Worked well! Never seen such a quick and efficient pack up!

Stan Atkinson was responsible for looking after the Transmitters at Mount Lofty. One day I was setting up links at Mount Lofty when Stan said he was going to see a doctor. He kept hearing a buzzing sound in his head. A few days later he was in hospital with a brain tumour and soon after he died.

Could the high radiation environment at Mount Lofty have caused the tumour?

They suspected a mobile phone could cause tumours! After that, I was more careful handling microwave transmitters.

Health and Safety was always an important consideration on OBs:

- Children like to climb scaffolding and ladders.
- Drunken adults can be even more of a problem.
- Cables are an obvious trip hazard.
- Electrical equipment and chemicals must be handled with care and stored in a safe place.
- The station must supply sufficient wet-weather jackets and gumboots for the crew.

The OB supervisor is responsible for the health and safety of the crew. Some First Aid knowledge is useful!

I looked forward to retirement.

A sad way to end thirty-eight years in television.

But I believe they were the best years of television. In the early days it was interesting and fun. Gradually television became a serious business. Now with networking, SAS is not much more than a relay station.

The job title of OB Supervisor didn't change in thirty-eight years but the job certainly did.

I began covering WAFL football with two black and white cameras and went on to covering AFL football with up to twelve colour cameras, two slow motion replay machines, stereo sound, data statistics, return links and several other extra items.

From Image Orthicon tubes to Plumbicons ... then CCDs ... from 4x3 to Widescreen and High Definition ... from Analog to Digital.

We went from Valves to Transistors to Integrated Circuits, to Large Scale Integrated Circuits, Microprocessors and Digital Technology.

The change from knapsack VHF radio for communications to handheld UHF radios and mobile phones was more than welcome!

OTHER MEMORIES

TUFFEY

Margie was at work and I had the day off, so I decided to spray weeds. I mixed some weedkiller in the knapsack sprayer and went into the paddock looking for weeds.

After a couple of hours spraying I ran out of spray so I returned to the house.

I expected the usual greeting from our Maltese dog, Tuffey, and possibly our cat as well, but there was silence. Then I called out her name and searched the house without success. After checking around the gardens I decided to call Margie. She immediately left work and raced home.

We searched the house, gardens and sheds together but got no response. Margie rang the neighbours and then the Stirling police station. The police officer said a man with a heavy accent and broken English reported finding a small white dog on Germantown Hill on Mount Barker Road, near our house.

The man said that he found the dog yesterday, but it was difficult to understand him. The police officer gave Margie the man's phone number and she called him. With difficulty she found out that the dog he found was a small white dog wandering along the main road near our house.

When she asked him, "When? Was it today?"

He said, "YES—TERDAY!"

Margie asked him to call out, "Tuffey". He did … and the reaction was immediate!

The man and his wife lived nearby and the dog was Tuffey. She must have followed me into the paddock.

I didn't lock her in the house, but nor did I recall seeing her while I was preparing to spray or going into the paddock. Maybe she wanted company!

It would have been difficult following me for more than a hundred metres in high grass, over a creek bed, through a Ringlock fence and onto a busy main road.

After that day I would lock Tuffey in the house if I was home alone and working outside!

IN THE DOG HOUSE

We have always had a dog in the house. They have all been faithful, obedient and good company.

One of the best was Mischka. She was a cross between a German Shepherd and a Golden Retriever – she had the intelligence of a German Shepherd with the temperament of a

Mischka, Ben and Matt

Golden Retriever. At the time, Margie and I were both working, Ben was at university and working part-time for a fitness group and Matthew was still at Pulteney Grammar School.

One day I finished work early so it had been arranged that I would pick up Matt after school. There had been a series of thunderstorms during the day and it rained almost continuously. When I picked Matt up he was thoroughly wet!

We went straight home on the freeway as quickly as we could under the conditions. When we arrived we expected to be met by Mischka. All we heard was the sound of steady rain. Once we were inside the house we called out her name but there was still no response.

Mischka was terrified of thunder and lightning and didn't like to be alone in a storm. She could have been hiding.

While Matt changed into dry clothes I began checking each room in the house. With umbrellas and wet weather coats we checked all sheds and gardens calling out her name, but there was no response. Because we had all left her alone, she may have panicked and set out to find us. Ben had been the last one to leave a few hours previously.

Matt and I set out in the car looking for Mischka. We drove slowly along the road to Verdun and back and we were about to look along Mount Barker Road to Bridgewater when we saw a dog of Mischka's size.

It disappeared behind a fence at Grumpy's, the Pizza Restaurant next to the Hahndorf exit from the Freeway. It was only a few hundred metres away from where we were and we would have passed it coming home. I raced to where we saw the dog and pulled up on the road in front of the restaurant. We got out of the car and called her name.

A few seconds later Mischka came from behind the restaurant and ran to us with tail wagging. She was wet through to the skin and shaking but obviously very happy to see us. We wrapped her in an old towel from the back of the car and helped her onto the back seat. At home we dried her off with towels and hair dryer.

SLITHER IN

Margie's mum, Ruth, was staying with us, but we were both out when she saw a brown snake in our sunroom!

It must have come in through the dog door. Ruth looked for some kind of weapon to kill the snake. She found an axe but didn't want to damage the new linoleum on the floor. When the snake moved onto the concrete floor of the laundry she struck the snake with the axe, chopping off part of its tail. The snake slithered under the washing machine – out of sight!

I was at work and Margie had gone to pick up our son Ben from kindergarten, so Ruth decided to sit and wait and keep an eye on the snake.

When Margie arrived home her mum explained what had happened. They poured themselves a stiff drink and kept an eye on the washing machine while Margie rang the police to ask for advice. The police officer said that the snake was a protected species and they weren't allowed to kill it, then suggested calling a snake catcher.

Our neighbour, Max, was very resourceful. He would know what to do!

A quick phone call and Max arrived with a piece of heavy gauge fencing wire. The wire was about four foot long with one end bent around to form a hook. Max said he always kept it by the back door … just in case!

Margie showed Max where the snake had last been seen. Max got down on his hands and knees to look under the washing machine but he couldn't see it. When he looked around he saw the snake under the bed just behind him.

Margie and her mum had been sitting on that bed! When had the snake moved?

Max caught the snake with the wire hook and dragged it out from under the bed, out the back door and onto the back lawn. A few blows from the fencing wire and the snake was dead.

We showed the dead snake to Ben, just so he would know what they look like. Immediately Ben wanted to take it to kindergarten to show the other kids. We looked for a suitable container to put the snake in to transport it to the kindy.

An old glass wine flagon was perfect!

The snake just fitted through the neck of the flagon and coiled up! It looked remarkably alive!

Ben was very excited the next morning when he arrived at kindergarten. He picked up the flagon and ran towards the entrance before any explanation had been given by Margie.

Unfortunately, Ben tripped and fell, dropping the flagon. The flagon broke and the dead snake fell out – uncoiling and still looking remarkably alive, sending parents and kids in all directions.

Ben cried out, "You told me it was dead!", adding to the confusion!

The kindergarten learnt a new rhyme that day, and used it to full advantage at the Christmas concert with their original presentation, "Snakes in the sunroom, hiss hiss hiss!"

SNAKES ALIVE

I was spraying blackberries alongside the main road and close to the creek, where the grass is very high and dense.

As luck would have it, I was wearing thick gumboots! Wouldn't go without them!

To get to one blackberry plant the grass was particularly thick. I couldn't see the ground in front of me. As I took a big step forward my foot seemed to drop into a hollow. At the same time I felt something move under my foot, so I took a giant leap backwards.

A large brown snake was attached to the toe of my gumboot. It let go of my boot and quickly retreated disappearing into the long grass.

When I checked my boot I found two fang marks surrounded by a damp patch … venom!

GOING BATTY

A female research student approached us for permission to look for bats on our property.

The 'Bat lady' (as the boys called her) found a number of small bats around one shed in particular.

She set up nets to trap the bats then brought them inside the house to check them, measure them and sex them. The result was the bats were all female or juveniles. We had a bat nursery!

One day we found a baby bat on the ground. It couldn't fly, so Margie hand-reared it.

We called the bat, Cricket!

Once he had grown a bit we encouraged him to learn to fly down the passageway of our house. When Cricket could fly with confidence we let him loose in the family room where he established a roost behind a painting hanging on the wall.

To feed Cricket we would pick up a mealworm between our fingers and hold it up high. While flying around the room, Cricket would swoop down and take the mealworm, then eat it while flying. Occasionally we would catch a moth for him.

When we decided to go to Kangaroo Island for a holiday we arranged for all of our animals to be fed, except Cricket.

We took Cricket with us, transporting him in a picnic basket. After returning from our holiday, one night someone left a door open and Cricket escaped. Let's hope he survived out there!

www.ingramcontent.com/pod-product-compliance
Ingram Content Group UK Ltd.
Pitfield, Milton Keynes, MK11 3LW, UK
UKHW062307290726
14090UKWH00018B/930